MDCCCCLV
EX LIBRIS
LYALL MORRILL, JR.

CONTENTS

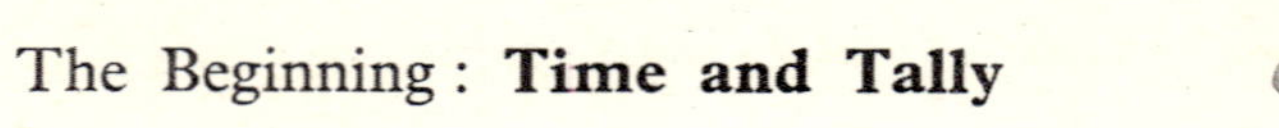

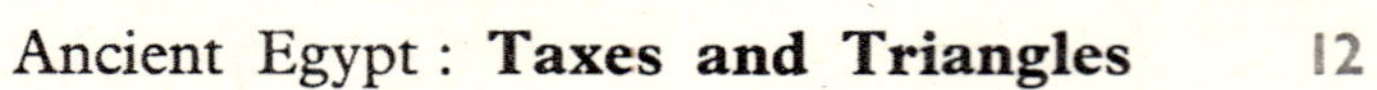

Library of Congress Card Catalog No. 55-10508

Produced by Rathbone Books, London – Printed in Great Britain by L. T. A. Robinson, Ltd., London

THE WONDERFUL WORLD OF MATHEMATICS

LANCELOT HOGBEN

Art by

André
Charles Keeping
Kenneth Symonds

maps by Marjorie Saynor

GARDEN CITY BOOKS GARDEN CITY NEW YORK

FIRST PUBLISHED IN THE UNITED STATES OF AMERICA IN 1955

Time and Tally

F*OR MY one deer you must give me three of your spearheads.* The earliest men and women like ourselves lived about twenty-five thousand years ago. They could say all this with their hands, simply by pointing one finger at the deer and three at the spearheads. The primitive way of counting with one finger for one thing and three fingers for three things, was the only kind of arithmetic they knew. For thousands of years such people thought of any quantity greater than three as a heap or pile.

They had no towns, no villages. They were wanderers who trekked from place to place in search of animals and birds to hunt and of berries, roots, and grain to gather. The only goods they possessed were the skins of animals, to protect them from the cold night air, a few hunting weapons, crude vessels to hold water, and perhaps some kind of lucky charm, such as a necklace of bear's teeth or sea-shells.

There was no need for them to know much arithmetic. Even their simple finger-counting was useful only on the rare occasions when they wanted to exchange goods with the members of some other tribe.

Every night, at places as far north as Great Britain you may see a star-cluster circle slowly round the Pole Star which scarcely moves.

Much more important to these hunters and food-gatherers was a knowledge of the seasons and of direction. Knowledge of the seasons could help them to forecast when the nuts and berries were beginning to ripen in some far-off forest, and a knowledge of direction would help them to find their way there. With neither calendars nor maps to help them they had to learn these things slowly, by long experience through trial and error.

While they were wandering through countryside they knew, they could find their way by remembering the positions of familiar hills, lakes and streams; but when drought or hunger drove them to seek new hunting grounds they had only the sun, moon and stars to guide them.

Tribes living near the sea might notice that the sun seemed to rise each morning out of the waves and set each night behind some distant line of hills. They could find their way to the sea by marching towards the rising sun, or to the hills by marching towards the setting sun. But this bit of knowledge would give them only a very rough-and-ready guide, for the sun's rising and setting positions change from season to season.

The stars of the night sky offered a much more reliable clue to direction but it must have taken many, many years for the wise men or women of these early tribes to discover it. We can imagine them, after the day's hunting was over, sitting by the opening of a shelter or the mouth of a cave and gazing up into the starlit sky. After a time they would notice certain clusters of stars that formed simple patterns which they could pick out night after night. These star-clusters seemed to trace part of a circular path across the sky, moving slowly round like the hands of some giant clock.

Some clusters seem to circle around a fixed point in the northern sky. There lies what we now call the North Pole Star, which scarcely changes its position in the night sky in a hundred years. Since it seems to be fixed, it is a kind of signpost. Nightlong this star shows us where what we call north lies, if we can spot it among all the hundreds of other stars that shine and twinkle in the sky.

Like us, the hunter of twenty-five thousand years ago could locate this signpost by spotting a cluster of seven stars, shaped rather like a big dipper or an ancient plough. This cluster circles around the Pole Star. Wherever we see it in the night sky, two of its stars point almost directly to the Pole Star. If we go the way they point, we are going northwards.

By night a man can rely on the Pole Star to guide him north.

From its full round, the moon changes a little every night, growing slimmer until it disappears, then gradually back to the full.

Sun, moon and stars were not only man's first signposts, they were also his first clock. During the day, the early hunter living north of the tropics would see the long morning shadows point westward. He would watch them grow gradually shorter until the sun reached its highest

The first calendar: notches cut to record changes of the moon.

point in the heavens at noon. As the sun sank lower, he would then see the shadows, now pointing eastward, slowly lengthen again. By noticing the length of shadow he could roughly tell what we now call the time of day.

Watching by the camp fire, these early folk would notice that the moon when full is highest in the sky just halfway through the night. In time, the more observant ones would also learn to judge the night hours by following the course of certain star-clusters which circle around the Pole Star.

To measure longer periods of time, our first forefathers must have relied on the moon. Night by night they saw how it gradually changes from a full disc of silver to a slim crescent and then disappears altogether. After a few dark nights, it reappears as a crescent and slowly grows again to its full size.

Just as the full moon was rising, a hungry tribe might pitch its tents near a wood whose boughs were laden with sour, green berries. The wise ones might say: Let us not touch these berries now; let us come back when the moon is once more full; then they will be black and good for plucking. The clan would then wander far afield in search of other food. Somehow they had to make sure of getting back at the right time. To do that, they would need to count the days.

Time flies, and counting days or months is not like counting dead deer or bear's teeth. We cannot make days stand in a row while we count them on our fingers. Our forefathers most likely first solved the problem by cutting a notch on a tree, a stick or a stone to mark the passage of each day: one notch – one day, two notches – two days, and so on. In time they would discover that there are always thirty days between one full moon and

Incas of Peru knotted cords called quipus for keeping count.

When man learned to herd cattle into natural pens and to sow and reap grain, he could stop wandering and live in a fixed home.

the next. So they might cut a bigger notch to mark a full moon. Twelve of these bigger notches would round off 360 days – roughly a year. We then have our first crude moon-calendar embracing the four seasons from spring to spring again.

After many thousands of years, some of these early hunters slowly began a new way of life. On returning to an old camping site, they would notice that grain left littered on their last visit was now sprouting in plenty. From this experience they learned to set some aside for planting. With the help of their constant companion, the dog, they also began to herd sheep, goats and cattle into ravines where it was easy to keep them penned in ready for slaughter only when there was need for meat. Instead of searching for wild herbs and berries, they sowed and reaped their own crops. They thus became shepherds and farmers.

As they settled down in villages they collected more and more goods which they could call their own. With hoes and digging-sticks, fields and fences, crops and herds, men needed to keep a record of their possessions. The earliest way of recording was the tally-system of the calendar-makers – one mark for one thing, two marks for two things, and so on. Counting this way lasted over a long period. In the New World, the Incas of Peru used to tie one knot in a cord to record each sheaf of grain gathered in at harvest, and in parts of the Old World there are still shepherds who cut chips in a stick when counting their flocks.

As men became farmers, they had to be able to forecast accurately the times of lambing and calving, of sowing and reaping. The hunter's rough-and-ready moon-calendar was no longer good enough. Nor was his way of recording numbers.

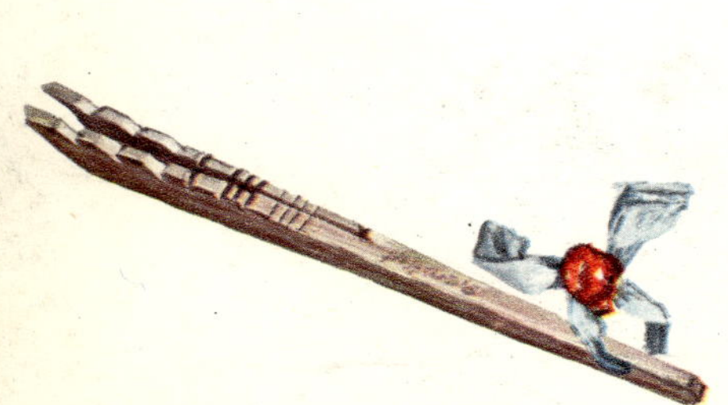

Tally stick: half of it formed a receipt in the Middle Ages.

Even today some European shepherds notch sticks when counting: one notch for ten sheep.

EGYPTIAN

I	II	III	IIII	IIIII	IIIIII	IIIIIII	IIIIIIII	IIIIIIIII	∩	𓍢	𓆼
1	2	3	4	5	6	7	8	9	10	100	1,000

BABYLONIAN

Y	YY	YYY	YYYY	YYYYY	YYYYYY	YYYYYYY	YYYYYYYY	YYYYYYYYY	<	Y	<
1	2	3	4	5	6	7	8	9	10	60	600

Early numbers show traces of notch-recording. Egyptians, Babylonians and Romans used strokes for the first few numbers and different signs for higher numbers.

EARLY ROMAN

I	II	III	IIII	V	VI	VII	VIII	VIIII	X	L	C	IↃ	CIↃ
1	2	3	4	5	6	7	8	9	10	50	100	500	1,000

Two six-hundreds, four sixties, five tens, two.

One thousand, four hundreds, nine tens, two.

CIↃ CCCC L XXXX II

One thousand, four hundreds, one fifty, four tens, two.

If the farmer uses a moon-calendar of 360 days to forecast the seasons, he will make an error of five days the first year, ten days the next year and so on. Thus the wise men who were able to work out a sun-calendar, which is accurate, became people of special importance. Farmers willingly provided them with a living, so that they could devote their time to foretelling the seasons.

As time passed, the calendar-specialists became a ruling class. More often than not they were also priests, who offered sacrifices to appease the gods of drought or storm and made thankofferings to the gods of harvest and abundance.

Though they thus mixed magic with their calendar-making, they did their job with surprising skill. Day by day they noted how the sun's rising position changed throughout the seasons; night by night they marked which star-clusters shone in the western sky where the sun had just set. In time they measured the length of the year to within an hour or two accurately. Without written records they could never have remembered all that their careful work taught them.

The earliest written numbers we know of were used in Egypt and Mesopotamia about five thousand years ago. Although these two lands are many miles apart, both their number systems seem to have started in the same way, by chipping notches on wood or stone to record the passing days. The priests of Egypt wrote on papyrus made from reeds, those of Mesopotamia on soft clay. So the shapes of their numbers are naturally different; but both used simple strokes for ones and different marks for tens and higher numbers.

一千四百九十二

1 × 1,000, 4 × 100, 9 × 10, 2

CHINESE

一	二	三	四	五	六	七	八	九	十	百	千
1	2	3	4	5	6	7	8	9	10	100	1,000

The Mayas of Central America, cut off from the Old World, developed farming, building and time-reckoning in their own way.

MAYA

1 2 3 4 5 6 7 8 9 10

20 40 60 80 100 120 140 160 180 200

Just as our 0 makes a number ten times larger, Maya made it twenty times larger.

Both built up the number they wanted simply by repeating the strokes and marks as often as necessary.

Three thousand years later the Romans still made strokes for the numbers one to four. They used new signs, in the form of letters, for fives, tens, fifties and so on. At about the same time, the people of China used a different sign for every number up to ten but still used strokes for the first three numbers.

The most remarkable of all early number systems was that used by the Mayas of Central America. Completely cut off from the civilisations of the Old World, these people could write any number with the help of only three signs – a dot, a stroke and a kind of oval. With dots and strokes only, they could build up any number from one to nineteen ( ). By adding one oval below any number, they made it twenty times larger, thus: •=1; =20. Adding a second oval would again multiply the number by twenty. In time-reckoning, however, they adjusted this system: adding a second oval multiplied the number by eighteen instead of twenty, so that meant *not* 400 (1 × 20 × 20) but 360 (1 × 20 × 18). If we recall the moon-calendar of 360 days, we can understand why they used their number signs in this way.

In time the Mayas used a sun-calendar of 365 days. For their records of dates, carved on stone columns called steles, they used special numerals shaped like human faces.

Maya stele.

Taxes and Triangles

THE PRIESTS of early Egypt became the most powerful men in the land. It was they who fixed the many holy days – days when the feasts of the full moon or of the midsummer sun were to be held, days when animals sacred to certain star-clusters were to be sacrificed, days when offerings were to be made to the gods of the river. It was they, too, who ordered the building of great temples, which they also used as observatories, and of the mighty pyramids, which served as the tombs for their rulers, the Pharaohs.

To erect such stupendous buildings, the architects of Egypt had to know how to make some kind of ground-plan, how to level the edges of stone blocks, how to haul them up from the ground, and how to set them fairly and squarely in position. In learning all this, the pyramid architects were making practical discoveries in the art of measurement, or as we now say, geometry.

The first ground-plans, forerunners of our own blueprints, were probably drawn on clay, simple diagrams to show the shape of the finished building. Those who made them had indeed learned that two things – a drawing and a building – may be of quite different size but of exactly the same shape. So what is true about the shape of one is also true about the shape of the other.

When the ground-plan was complete, men with hoes levelled off a stretch of land ready for the masons to begin work. There were as yet neither wheeled vehicles nor good roads. Cargoes of heavy building materials, consisting mainly of stone blocks weighing several tons, came as near to the site as possible along the River Nile by boat.

Each block of stone had to be cut to shape. First the rough edges were knocked off with lumps of flint. Next the surfaces were levelled with metal chisels and bell-shaped wooden mallets. Last of all the whole block was smoothed by rubbing with a rough stone tool. Every corner had to be tested with a mason's square, or set-square, to make sure it was a true right-angle.

Then an enormous layer of blocks was laid to form the base of the pyramid. On this a second layer was built, slightly smaller and exactly in the middle of the first. Layer after layer was added in the same way so that all four sides of the finished pyramid would taper equally and meet neatly at the top. To check that it was upright, the edge of each had to be tested with a weight hanging from a string. Earth was piled up the step-like edges to make a sloping road over which the blocks were hauled on sledges with rollers beneath them.

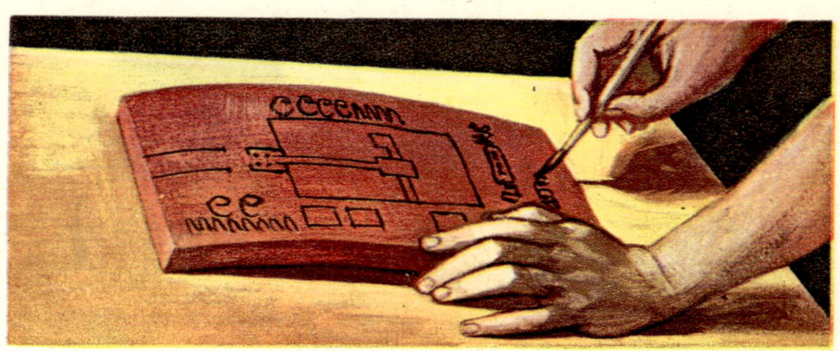

Scale plans were drawn on clay tablets before building began.

Each block was shaped and corner tested with mason's square.

Heavy blocks were hauled up sand ramps on sledges, over rollers.

Plumb-line checked that the blocks were set exactly upright.

Perhaps the hardest problem was to make the base of the pyramid really square. The smallest error in fixing the angle at any corner would have thrown the whole building out of shape. Although the builders left no records, we may guess how they would do this.

They might mark out a long straight line, by stretching a cord between two pegs stuck in the ground. Then to each peg they would tie an equal length of string, more than half as long as the line they had drawn. By keeping these strings stretched tight and moving the ends around, they could draw parts of two perfect circles. These part-circles we call arcs will cross each other at two points. When the builder draws a straight line between these two points, he will find it bisects the original line, that is it crosses it at a right-angle, cutting it into two equal parts.

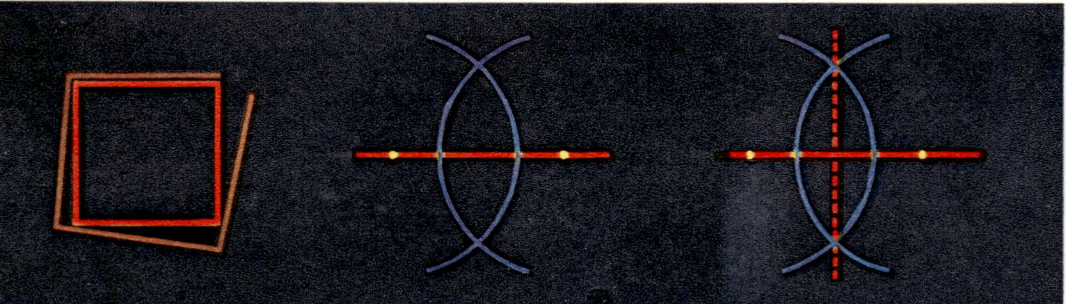

One false angle at base would ruin the shape. Right-angles can be made by drawing equal arcs from any two spots on a straight line, and joining the points where the arcs cross.

The builders of ancient Egypt checked that their walls were built at right-angles to the ground by means of a plumb-line.

The builder must be able to mark out right-angles on the flat ground to get his foundations square. To test whether his walls are dead upright, he also needs to make right-angles in the air. For this purpose, the Egyptian builders used the plumb-line, a device we still use today. If the plumb-line is suspended from the top of a wall so that the weight is free to swing, it traces an arc of a circle, and comes to rest at right-angles to the ground. If level with it, the wall is vertical.

When plumb-line stops swinging, it grazes the ground at right angles.

Of all ways of drawing a right-angle the simplest is to use a set-square. The Egyptians did so. But first they had to *make* one, and to do this they had first to make a right-angled triangle.

Who first made this discovery we may never know. Possibly it was the professional rope-knotters whose job it was to tie equally-spaced knots in the long ropes used for measuring. Somehow they found that pegging out certain lengths of rope in the form of a triangle produces a right-angle opposite the longest side. Taking a length as the space between two knots, one combination that gives this result is 3 lengths, 4 lengths and 5 lengths. Another is 5, 12 and 13. By cutting pieces of wood of such lengths and by joining them end to end, they could make a set-square.

Crude ways of measuring, good enough for their forefathers, were not good enough for these builders of great temples and pyramids. The farmer who set out to build a stone or wooden hut with his own hands could say: My hut will

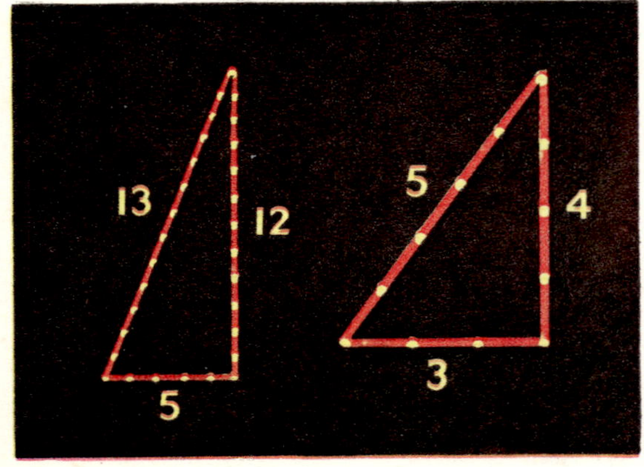

A triangle with sides 3, 4 and 5 lengths has a right-angle opposite its longest side: so has one with sides 5, 12 and 13 lengths.

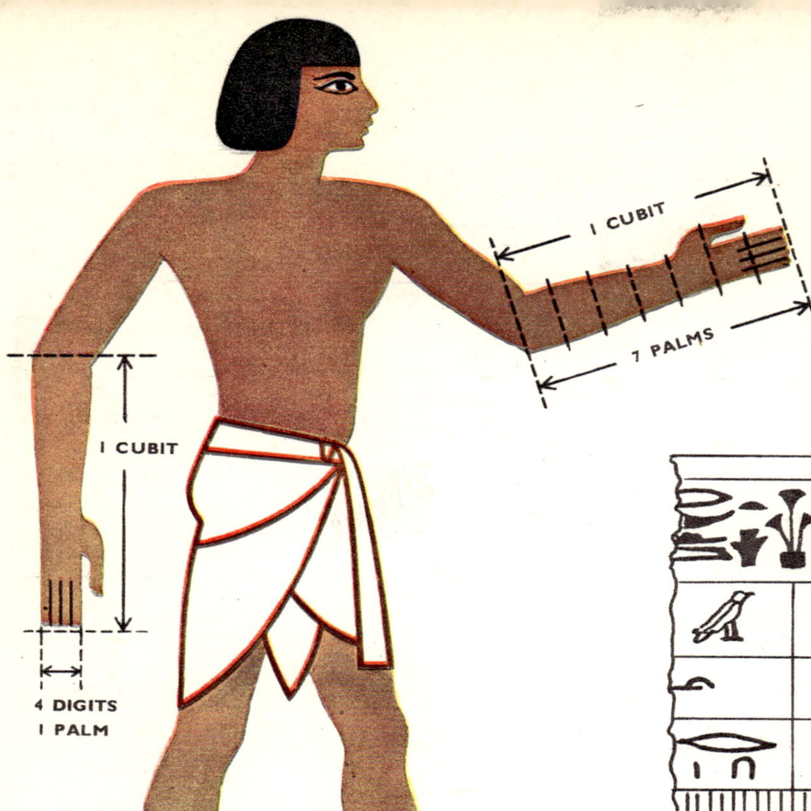

Early measures were based on the proportions of a man's body.

Part of an Egyptian measure, with marks for fractions.

Egyptian fractions were always one part of something. The sign for 'one part of' was ⬭. Fractions shown below are 1/10 (⬭), 1/9 (⬭), 1/8 (⬭) and 1/7 (⬭).

Museo Egizio, Turin

be six paces long and four paces wide, the roof will be a hand-span higher than the crown of my head. The temple architect could not give building instructions in paces and spans. Every workman under him might have a different pace and span.

For large-scale building there had thus to be measures that were always the same, no matter who did the measuring. In the beginning they were commonly based on the proportions of one man's body, possibly a king's. These standard measures were fixed by rulers of wood or metal.

In Egypt the main standard of length was the cubit, often mentioned in the Bible. It was the length of a man's forearm from the elbow to the tip of the outstretched middle finger. There were also smaller measures: the palm, one-seventh of a cubit, and the digit, one-quarter of a palm.

Such smaller units were very important to the Egyptians because they found fractions hard to handle. We now think easily of fractions such as three-fifths, or nine-tenths, but a fraction to an Egyptian was always one part of something. It was too hard to think of three-sevenths of a cubit but not by any means difficult to talk of three palms.

These early measures seem strange at first, but equally strange ones are still in use. A Briton or an American still measures his own height in feet. He still says 'seven inches' to avoid using the fraction 'seven-twelfths of a foot'.

At harvest time each year the priests of Egypt levied payment for their services by collecting taxes from the farmers who paid in goods. To fix the payment due, there had to be standard jars for measuring out grain, wine or oil, and standard weights for weighing other produce.

Scales were used for weighing, jars for measuring.

British Museum

Before gathering taxes the priests measured the area of each field. Odd-shaped fields were first marked off into triangles.

It seems that the amount of tax depended on the size of the farm; the bigger the farm, the bigger the tax. To levy taxes, the priests therefore needed some way of measuring area.

Perhaps their first clue to area-measurement came when paving the floor of a temple with square tiles. A strip of floor six tiles long and six wide needs thirty-six tiles (6 × 6) to cover it. Another strip, ten tiles long and four wide, needs forty (10×4). To find the area of a square or oblong, you merely multiply its length by its width.

But not all fields were square or oblong. The tax-gatherer would come upon fields that seemed all sides and corners. There was no way of dividing them into squares, but he *could* easily divide them into triangles. If he knew how to find the

Base 3, height 3. Area 9.

A square folds into two triangles. Each is half the area of the square.

Base 5, height 3. Area 15.

An oblong cuts into two triangles. Each is half the area of oblong.

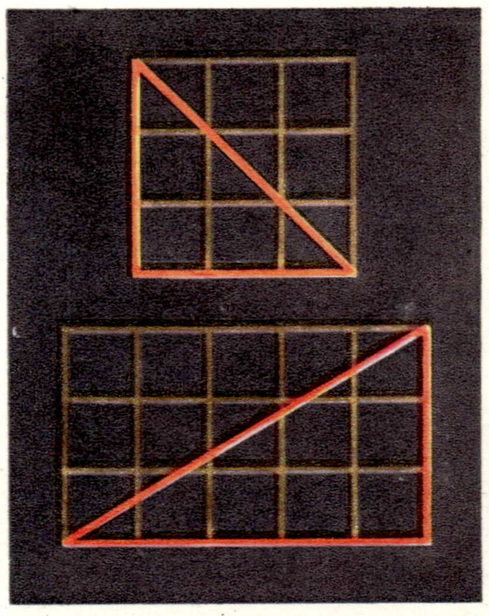

The area of any right-angled triangle is half the area of the square or oblong with the same base and height.

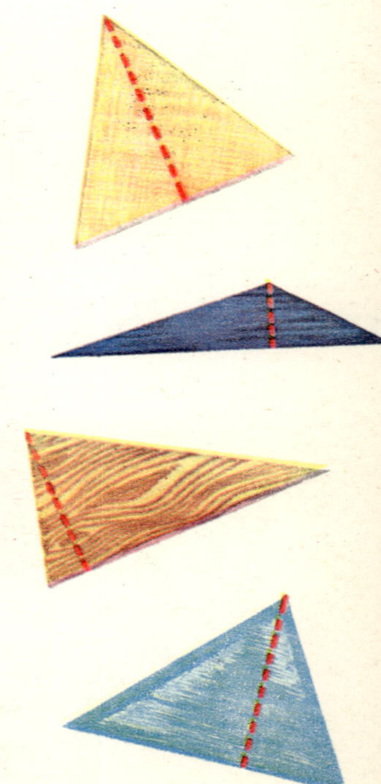

area of a triangle he could thus measure *any* field, providing its sides were all straight.

Happily it is only a short step to learn how to find the area of a triangle once you know how to find the area of a square or an oblong. A square piece of linen will fold into two equal triangles, each half the size of the square. An oblong piece will cut into two equal triangles, each half the size of the oblong. Possibly such simple clues gave the priests a guide to the rule they needed. They saw that we find the area of a triangle by multiplying its base (or length) by its height (or width) and dividing the answer by two.

The job of measuring the fields kept the priests busier than we might think. The farmland of Egypt lies in a narrow strip near the great River Nile. On either side of this fertile strip, all is desert. At midsummer each year the river overflows its banks, watering the nearby land and leaving behind a thin layer of rich, muddy soil when the floods go down again. This yearly flooding helped the early farmers of Egypt to

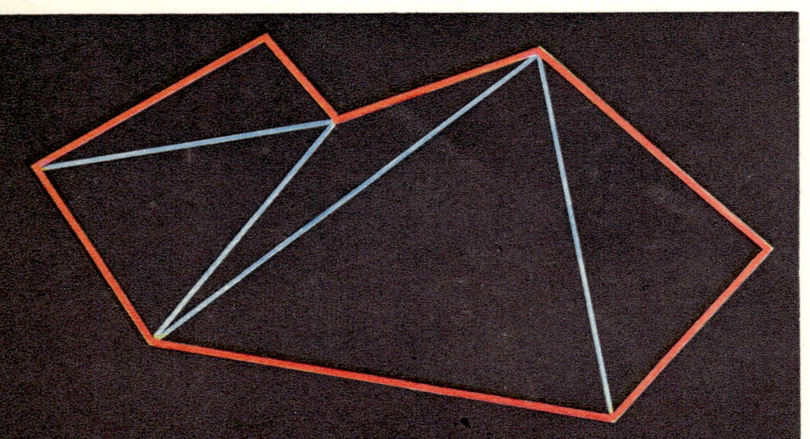

By measuring every triangular strip we can find the total area.

grow fine crops, but it also washed away the boundary-marks between their fields. So the priests had to measure each plot of land again and again, year in and year out. They were not merely calendar-makers and architects. They were also the world's first professional surveyors.

Ever since the days of the Egyptians, the main working method used by surveyors of all ages has been what they call triangulation. When we think about how much the early priest-surveyors must have learned about the shapes and areas of triangles, we begin to see how much the mathematicians of later times gained from their practical knowledge. To it, we owe the very word geometry, made up

Food grows only where the Nile floods. Beyond, all is desert.

from two Greek words, one meaning earth or land and the other measurement.

Of course, the surveyor meets problems that he cannot solve by the simple rule for finding the area of the triangle. He cannot mark out a circle in strips which are exactly triangular.

The early Egyptians almost certainly drew circles by pulling a tightly stretched cord around a fixed peg. They knew they must use a long cord to draw a large circle and a short cord to draw a small one. They knew, in fact, that the area of a circle depends on the distance from its middle-point to its edge, or on what we now call its radius.

About 3,500 years ago, when the great pyramids were already very old, an Egyptian scribe named Ahmes, the Moonborn, put a rule about this in writing. The area of a circle is very nearly three and one-seventh times as great as the area of a square drawn on its radius. That is, if the radius is 3 inches, the area of the circle is roughly $3\frac{1}{7} \times 9$ square inches. How the priests made this discovery we may never know. In the British Museum in London hangs the carefully framed papyrus manuscript written by Ahmes himself. Unfortunately it gives us no explanation.

Symbol for radiance

Finding North and South

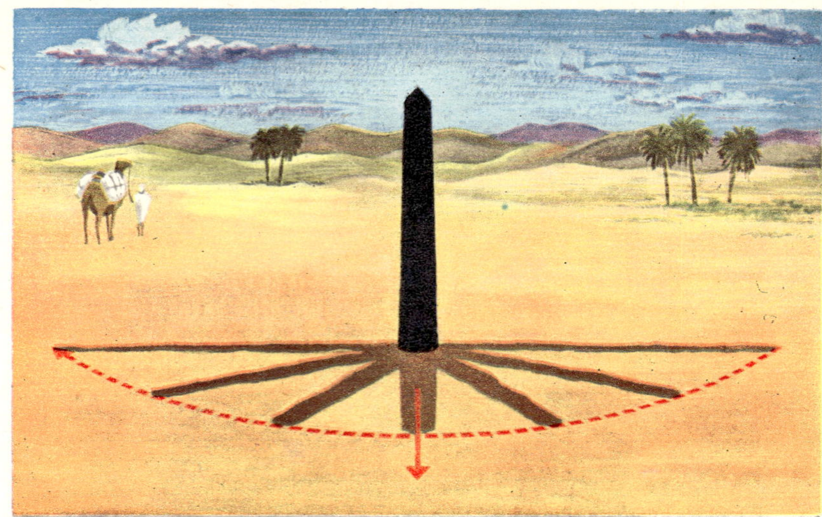

North of the Tropic of Cancer, the sun's noon shadow points always due north.

Finding East and West

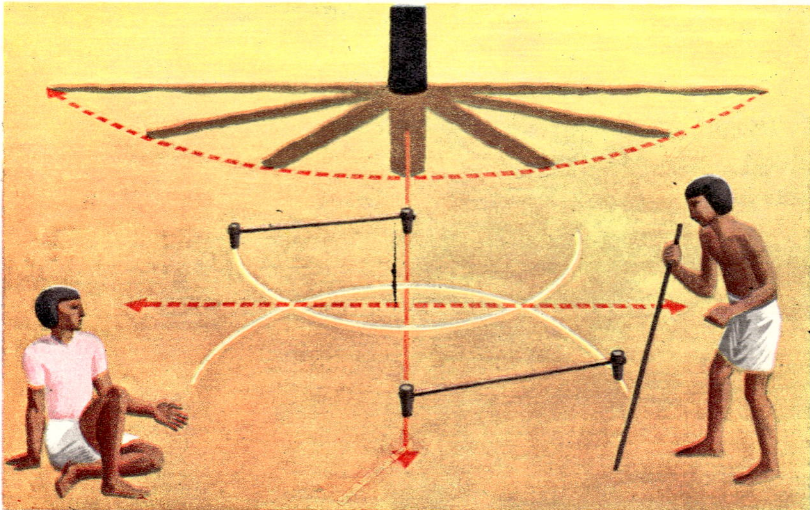

A line drawn at right-angles to the noon shadow points due east and west.

Ra, God of the Sun, holds the sceptres of east and west.

The temple at Karnak was built in such a way that at dawn on midsummer's day a man looking along the line of columns would see the rising sun straight ahead.

At dawn this Egyptian sundial was set with its crossbar facing towards the east. The longest shadow marked the sixth hour before noon. At mid-day, when the shadow was shortest, the dial was turned round. Slowly the shadow lengthened and marked the afternoon hours.

Scattered in museums around the world there are other early manuscripts which give us a glimpse into the mathematics of Egypt, but most of our knowledge comes from examining the ancient buildings which still stand near the Nile.

We can tell how accurately the priestly architects could fix direction from the fact that the four faces of certain pyramids look precisely toward north, south, east and west. The architects probably found north and south from the noon shadow of some tall column. By drawing a line at right-angles to such a shadow, they could place east and west as well.

There is also another way of finding east which the Egyptians must have understood. Day by day, the sun's rising position gradually changes. In winter it rises to the south of east, in summer to the north of east. If you can halve the angle between its midwinter and midsummer rising positions you will know what is due east.

By counting the days between two occasions when the sun reached its most northerly rising position, the Egyptians could measure the length of the year. At Karnak they built a temple with a line of columns pointing to where the sun rose on midsummer's day. Only once in 365 days did the rising sun shine straight along that line.

In finding direction and measuring time, the Egyptian had only the same clues as the hunters and food-gatherers of a bygone age: the rising and setting positions of sun, moon and stars, the shadow of the sun by day and the rotation of star-clusters around the Pole Star at night. Years of careful recording, however, enabled the Egyptian to make far better use of these clues. The early hunter looking at the long shadow cast by a tree could say at best: It is still early morning. The Egyptian, with a sun-clock which measured the length of a shadow falling on a marked strip of wood, could look at the shadow and say: The second hour of morning is at hand.

Here we have real science; but many of the priestly drawings of ancient Egypt show the gods busy controlling the points of the compass or the hours of day and night. Along with real science they trailed a heavy load of superstition.

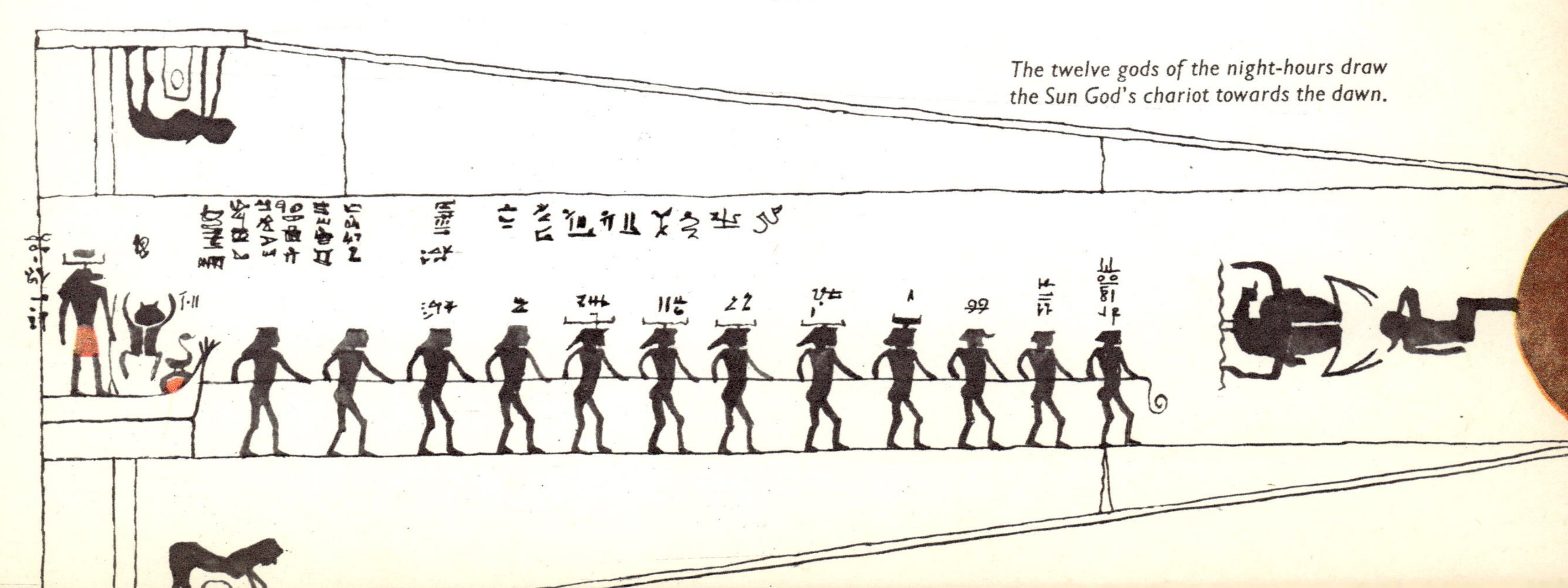

The twelve gods of the night-hours draw the Sun God's chariot towards the dawn.

Square and Circle

A THOUSAND miles east of the delta of the River Nile are two other great rivers, the Tigris and Euphrates. Between and beside their banks, in the land called Mesopotamia, there grew up another civilisation, at least as ancient as that of Egypt.

Historians refer to this civilisation at different stages of its development as Sumerian, Chaldean, Assyrian and Babylonian. It was in some ways very similar to the Egyptian. In both, the priestly sky-watchers and calendar-keepers were the ruling class and both made astonishing progress in astronomy. By about 2000 B.C. the priests in these lands had built up temple-libraries where they recorded their knowledge in a secret script which ordinary men could not read.

There the resemblance between the two civilisations ends.

Mesopotamia, unlike early Egypt, had a considerable foreign trade. It had no wood of its own suitable for building, no silk of its own to clothe kings and princes, no spices for the dishes of the wealthy, few precious metals from which to make vessels for the temples. To meet all these needs, merchants with caravans of asses or camels travelled through mountain pass and over desert, going westward to Lebanon for cedar-wood, northward into Asia Minor for gold, silver, lead or copper, and eastward possibly as far as India and China for silks, dyes, spices and jewels.

A merchant, selling the produce of his fields, may be content to measure his wares roughly and to sell them by the donkey-load; but a merchant dealing in more costly goods needs to be far more precise.

Thus, in Mesopotamia, scales and standard weights came into common use, and the merchant weighed his heavy goods in talents (roughly fifty-five pounds) and his precious wares in shekels (rather less than one-third of an ounce). But the merchant also needed to find something which anyone and everyone would accept as payment for goods. There was one thing which almost everybody would accept: barley. For many

Later, the merchants learned to use scales and standard weights.

Assyrian lion weights.

Early Babylonians weighed and sold their goods by the donkey-load.

Still later, standard weights of silver were used as money.

years, barley was the workman's wage. What was left over after he had made his bread and brewed his beer he could exchange for other things. So the early Mesopotamian merchants, when they set off to trade with other lands, loaded their asses and camels with barley to pay for the goods they intended to buy.

As time went on they discovered that silver, much lighter and easier to handle than barley, would also be acceptable almost everywhere. At first, they would carry small quantities of it and weigh it out as necessary. Later, they side-stepped the constant trouble of weighing by casting small bars of silver each stamped to show its weight. Although not much like our modern coins in appearance, they were the world's first money.

Here, for the first time, was a kind of wealth which a man could save without fear that it would go bad. He could also lend it out and charge interest on it, as the usurers of the Bible story did. To do this, as when buying or selling, he would need to keep accounts.

In this task, the merchants of Mesopotamia were handicapped by a clumsy script and bulky writing material. They wrote with pointed sticks on tablets of soft clay; and they had to bake the tablets hard in the sun to hold the impression. The process must have slowed down writing considerably, but it made the finished tablets difficult to destroy. In recent years archaeologists have found thousands of them with wedge-shaped signs, called cuneiform, still clearly written on them.

It needed masterly detective-work to decipher the writing, partly because the signs, at first sight, all look very much alike, partly because different scribes used signs in different ways.

What stood for 10 in one place might stand for 60 in another; what stood for 100 (10 × 10) on one tablet might mean 3,600 (60 × 60) on the next.

Although Mesopotamia had elaborate systems of weights and measures, and although it was the first home of money, its methods of keeping written accounts remained at a very crude level. Fortunately for them, however, the merchants had a way of calculating without written numbers.

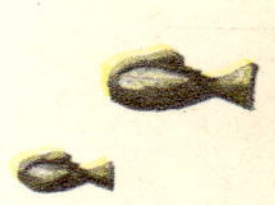

Babylonian duck weights.

Between two great rivers lies cradle of many civilisations.

The early scribes did their calculations on an abacus—pebbles in grooves in the sand. They recorded the results on clay tablets.

Like the Egyptians, they set out pebbles in grooves in the sand, each pebble in the first groove standing for one, each in the second groove for ten, each in the third for a hundred, and so on. The diagrams below show how the merchants used this device, called the abacus, for adding up their accounts, long before there were any rules for written arithmetic.

Notice how the number-value of a pebble grows as you move it from groove to groove: 1 in the first groove, 10×1 in the second, 10×10×1 in the third, 10×10×10×1 in the fourth. When

100's 10's 1's

To add 579 to 152, first place pebbles to show 579: 5 hundreds, 7 tens, 9 ones.

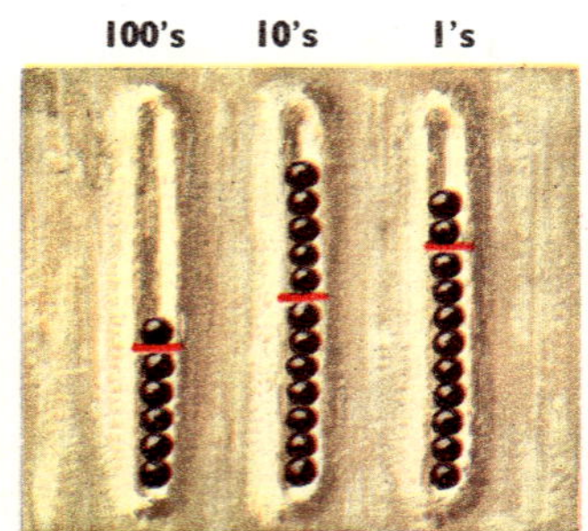

Add pebbles to show 152: 1 hundred, 5 tens, 2 ones. Ones column has 11 pebbles.

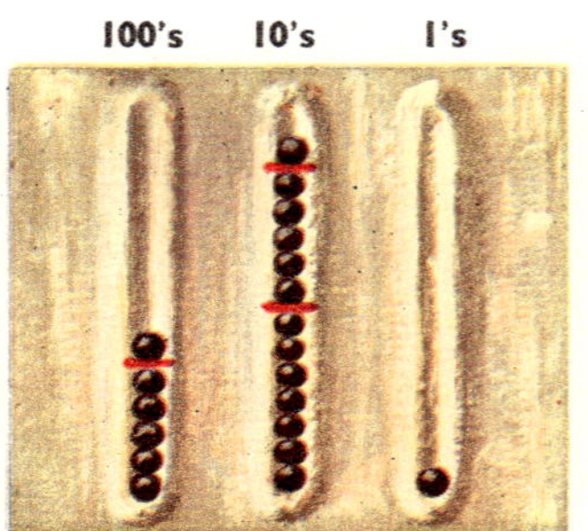

Carry 1 from ones column to tens, throw 9 out, leave 1. Tens column now has 13.

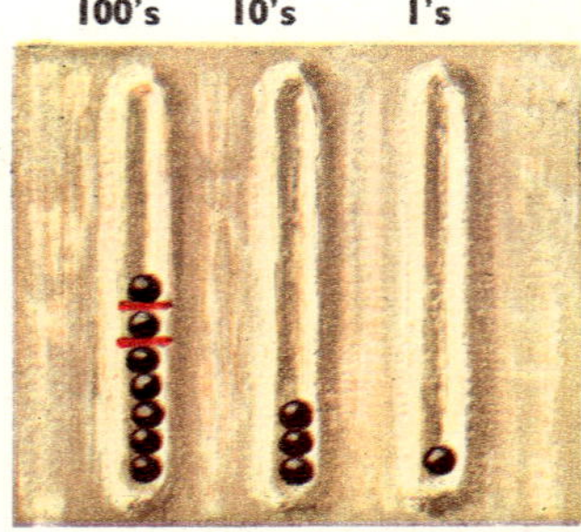

Carry 1 from tens to hundreds, throw 9 out, leave 3. Pebbles now give answer, 731.

the value of a pebble in each groove or column is ten times greater than in the one before it, we now say that ten is the base.

Most ancient number systems used a base of ten, probably because most people first learned to count on the fingers of their two hands. But there is nothing magic about the number ten. It is just as easy to work with a quite different base.

The Egyptians used ten as a base, and consistently used separate signs for 1, 10, 100, 1000 and so on, repeated to recall the number of pebbles in the corresponding groove. Although the people of Mesopotamia also used a base of ten, they sometimes used a base of sixty. A trace of this has come down to us. In measuring time, we still divide the hour into sixty minutes and the minute into sixty seconds. Navigators, in measuring distance, still divide each degree of longitude or latitude into sixty minutes, and each minute into sixty seconds. The Mayas of Central America, who may have used both toes and fingers for counting, used a base of twenty except in time-reckoning.

Mesopotamia was not the only country handicapped by clumsy signs for numbers. The same thing was true of most civilised lands until a few centuries ago, and so the habit of using the abacus spread in course of time over most of the world.

The abacus used in ancient Rome was a metal plate with two sets of parallel grooves, one below the other. The lower set held four pebbles in each groove and the upper set only one. The pebble in an upper groove was worth five times as much as a pebble in the corresponding lower groove. Thus the operator could show any number up to nine in each complete column. At the right of the metal plate there was a separate set of grooves used for working with fractions. The word the Romans used for a pebble was *calculus*, from which we get our own word calculate.

The abacus was not the only short-cut to calculation known to the merchants and traders of Mesopotamia. Among the thousands of clay tablets which archaeologists have unearthed from a temple library near the banks of the Euphrates, some are tables of multiplication and addition, and others are tables of the squares of numbers. The

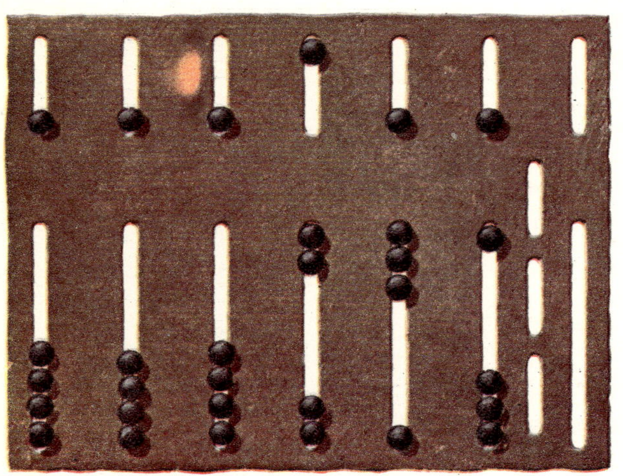

Roman bronze abacus. Beads in the top row count five.

square of a number simply means a number multiplied by itself, such as $2 \times 2 = 4$ which we now write as 2^2, or $5 \times 5 = 25$, which we now write as 5^2.

It seems likely that the priests of those days had discovered a way of using square tables which enabled them to multiply any two numbers together without using the abacus. Here, for example, is how they would multiply 102 by 96.

STEP 1 Add 102 to 96 and divide the result by 2 to find the average 99
STEP 2 Take 96 from 102; divide the result by 2, to find half the difference between the two numbers 3
STEP 3 Look up in the table the square of 99 and you at once see it is 9801
STEP 4 Look up in the table the square of 3 and you at once see it is 9
STEP 5 Take 9 from 9801 and you find the correct answer 9792

If we understand this method, we can multiply

Japanese businessmen still use the abacus with great skill.

any two numbers together in the same way. When we multiply one number by another, the result is always equal to the square of their average minus the square of half the difference between them. Yet square-table multiplication was never as widespread as the use of the abacus. Long after the time of Columbus, some merchants and shop-keepers of western Europe still used counting-boards worked on much the same principle as the abacus. The modern Chinese, Japanese and Russian businessman frequently uses the abacus today and works with great speed.

	1	2	3	4	5	6	7
1	1	2	3	4	5	6	[illegible]
2	2	4	6	8	10	12	14
3	3	6	9	12	15	18	2[illegible]
4	4	8	12	16	20	24	2[illegible]
5	5	10	15	20	25	30	3[illegible]
6	6	12	18	24	30	36	4[illegible]
7	7	14	[illegible]	28	35	42	[illegible]

Square table shows the results of multiplying numbers by themselves.

Part of the above, Babylonian style.

Wheel helped the potter to work faster and better.

About six thousand years ago some unknown citizen of ancient Mesopotamia made one of the greatest inventions of all time, the wheel. At first it was no more than a solid disc of wood with a hole in the middle to allow it to revolve round a fixed axle. By the time the Babylonians and Assyrians built their trading carts and war chariots it had become much more like the wheel of the farm cart still seen today, with rim, spokes and hub.

Mesopotamia found other uses for the wheel, too. By placing his clay on a turning wheel, the potter could mould his vessels more accurately. With the help of pulley-wheels, builders and engineers could raise heavy weights more easily.

It is tempting to suppose that the Mesopotamians, with their knowledge of wheels, learned a good deal about the geometry of the circle; but in fact they made no more progress than the Egyptians—probably not as much. The Egyptians estimated that the boundary, or circumference, of a circle is 3.14 times as long as its diameter. Since this ratio of circumference to diameter (or of area to square of radius), now called by the Greek letter π (prounced pi) is approximately 3.1416, this was quite a close estimate. The Mesopotamians were

The pulley-wheel made it possible to raise heavy weights.

commonly content to use the more convenient but less precise value, 3.0.

How these early peoples arrived at any value for π, however crude, is not certain; but some of their inscriptions give us a clue. By drawing the smallest square that can enclose a circle and the largest that can fit inside it, they could see that the boundary of a circle lies between the boundaries of the two squares, and it happens that the average boundary

of the two squares is almost $3\frac{1}{7}$ times the diameter of the circle. By drawing one hexagon outside, and another inside the circle, they could have obtained an even better estimate.

If the priests of Mesopotamia knew less about the circle than did those of Egypt, their knowledge of practical geometry was not inferior. In astronomy, also, they were as far advanced as the Egyptians. A work on astrology, prepared for Sargon, King of Babylon, almost five thousand years ago, includes a long list of the times of eclipses.

It is easy to understand why the sky-watchers of those days were so interested in eclipses. Astrology was a strange mixture of science and magic. The priests claimed that they could foretell from their observation of the heavens all kinds of things—the outcome of battles, the fortunes of kings, the wrath of the gods. If the priest could forecast eclipses with accuracy, people were more ready to listen to other prophecies he might make and to give him more power.

We now know that an eclipse of the moon occurs when the earth is in a straight line between sun and moon. The earth then casts a shadow across the moon's face. The priests of Mesopotamia forecast eclipses of the moon with sufficient reliability to make us think that they too probably knew this.

The astronomers of Babylon were keen observers of eclipses.

Babylonian map shows the earth as a disc.

British Museum

Half sum of outer and inner figures gives size of circle roughly.

This clay tablet shows early interest in square and circle.

Looking up at the round edge of the shadow on the partly-eclipsed moon, they would then realise that the earth itself must be round. Babylonian scribes did indeed draw fanciful maps of an earth whose shape was like a penny. On one such map which archaeologists have found in recent times, Babylon occupies a large area in the middle.

The Phoenicians ventured northwards to islands off Britain for tin.

They sailed south to the coast of western Africa for spices.

Stars and Steering

AROUND 1500 B.C. a large sea trade sprang up along the coast of Syria, in the land the Bible calls Phoenicia. From the great ports of Tyre and Sidon, Phoenician seamen sailed the length and breadth of the Mediterranean, fetching and carrying goods for most of the known world. The Old Testament prophet, Ezekiel, gives a picture of Tyre at the height of its power: Tyrus, thou art situate at the entry of the sea, a merchant of the people for many isles. Thy builders have made all thy ship boards of fir trees of Senir : they have taken cedars from Lebanon to make masts for thee. Fine linen with broidered work from Egypt was thy sail. Tarshish was thy merchant by reason of all kind of riches ; with silver, iron, tin and lead they traded in thy fairs.

Far off, tip of ship or island shows; from nearer, about half.

Nearer their homeland, the merchant-mariners went to Greece for cargoes of wine and olives; to Egypt for grain and linen.

With so many people flocking to buy their goods, ambitious sea-traders were tempted to send fleets on even longer voyages. By 1000 B.C. their ships had probably ventured into the Atlantic for tin from the Isles of Scilly, near Britain, and southward along the coast of Africa for spices.

In the course of their travels, the Phoenician mariner-merchants met the less advanced folk of Europe and of the Atlantic coast of Africa as well as the more civilised peoples of Egypt and of Mesopotamia. Their ships that plied the seas carried from one place to another valuable knowledge as well as valuable cargoes; and the long voyages also taught them much that the Egyptians and Mesopotamians had no opportunity of learning about the earth and the heavens.

People who live on or near the sea soon grow familiar with notions which would never occur to those who live inland. The citizen of Babylon or Nineveh would probably have laughed if an astrologer had tried to convince him that the earth is spherical; but the men of Tyre and Sidon could find it out for themselves.

A merchant watching for a ship to come into port, would first see the tip of a mast above the horizon, then the top half of a sail, and last of all the whole ship. A ship's lookout, if watching for some nearby island, would first see the top of its highest hill, then the lower slopes and finally the shore as well. It would be hard for either to explain what each saw without guessing that the curved surface of the earth hides the lower parts of distant objects from view.

Like most seafarers before the days of Columbus, the early Phoenicians seldom sailed farther than needs be from sight of land or familiar land-birds. In the long, narrow Mediterranean they could undertake east-west voyages of up to two thousand miles without long losing sight of a familiar coast or island. While the pilot could recognise such landmarks, he needed little knowledge of navigation as we now use the word.

Close up, whole is seen.

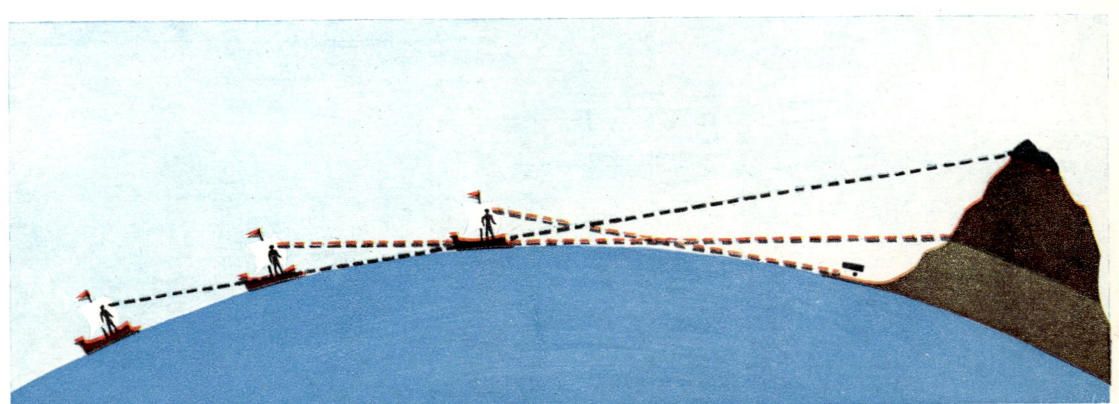

Thus the mariners learned that part of a distant view is hidden by the curved surface of the earth.

Phoenicians founded colonies all along the Mediterranean. From western ports they made north and south voyages in the Atlantic.

In time the Phoenicians founded colonies near the western end of the Mediterranean, including the great city-port of Carthage which became so powerful as to challenge the might of Rome to war three times in a single century. From these western colonies, mariners set out on voyages into the Atlantic. Sailing by strange shores with no familiar landmarks to guide them, they needed some way of reckoning how far north or south they had travelled.

Like the early hunters, they had to rely on the sun and on the stars; but they began with the advantage of already knowing something about astronomy. They soon learned more. Once pilots pushed out into the Atlantic and voyaged northward for tin, southward for spices, an entirely new picture of the changing heavens met their eyes. Along the European coast the noon sun, on any particular day, is lower in the sky at northern ports than at southern ones, and casts a longer shadow. The length of the noon shadow, different at different places on the same day of the year, gave the mariner his first daytime method of marking the latitude of a port on his crude map or chart. By night, a star close to where our North Pole Star now lies would equip him with another method. As a pilot sailed northward towards the Tin Isles he would see this star rise a little higher in the sky each night. As he sailed southward along the African coast he would see it dip night by night a little nearer to the horizon.

From earliest times men have noticed how sunbeam, moonbeam or starlight forms parallel straight lines. Slowly, the Phoenicians would connect their newly gained experience of the heavens in different latitudes with this age-old knowledge and realise that only one simple explanation fits the facts. That our earth is spherical can explain why such beams strike various parts of it at different angles at the same moment.

Noon shadows, long in the north, grow gradually shorter as one nears the Equator.

From very early times men have noticed how the rays of the sun are like parallel lines.

In northern seas the Pole Star is seen high overhead. Nearer to the Equator it seems to dip lower and lower towards the horizon. This changing angle gives the pilot a clue to his ship's north-south position.

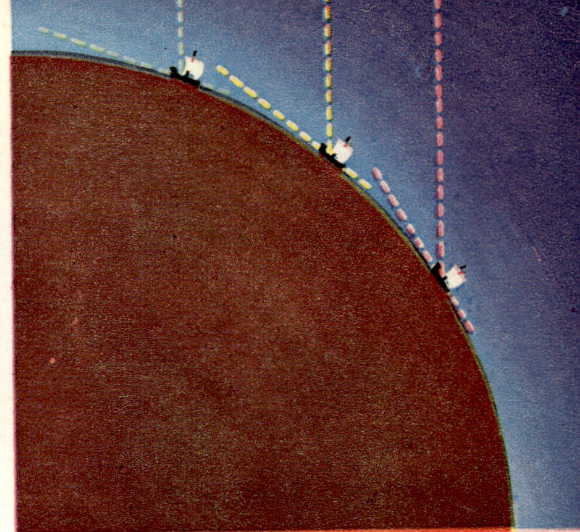

Other discoveries they made in their travels would strengthen this belief. In their own land the sun's noon shadow always points to the north, but on the Tropic of Cancer (about $23\frac{1}{2}$ degrees north) they would see the noonday sun at midsummer directly overhead, casting no shadow at all. Still farther south on the same day, the noon shadows point to the south.

On rare occasions, a captain would sail his ship far south along the coast of Africa. As he neared the Equator, he would see a star near the North Pole of the heavens very low in the sky. Farther south still he would lose sight of it altogether. Instead he would see bright stars and clusters which are never visible in northern lands.

The early pilots, with their new experience of the heavens, blazed a trail for a new science of navigation leading to further advances in the study of earth-measurement or geometry. During the early centuries of Mesopotamian civilisation, long before the time of the Phoenicians, man had learnt to divide the circle into 360 degrees. Now man was learning to divide the great circles which pass through the North and South Poles of the earth itself in the same way.

The mariner-merchants of Phoenicia and Carthage led the world in navigation for many years. As time went by Greek-speaking seamen of Sicily, Crete, Cyprus and many of the isles off the coast of Asia Minor, as well as what we now call Greece, challenged their leadership. By about 400 B.C. Greek geographers were beginning to draw charts on which the Mediterranean coastlines are recognisable.

But the Phoenicians left the Greeks a legacy far more valuable than such crude map-making. The men of Tyre and Sidon, who spoke a language rather like Hebrew, were among the earliest people to use a new sort of writing. Instead of using a vast number of picture-symbols for words or ideas, the Phoenicians used an alphabet made up of a few simple signs which stand for sounds. About 600 B.C. the Greeks adapted such an alphabet to their own very different language. Thereafter it was an easy matter to master the art of reading and the written word was no longer a secret.

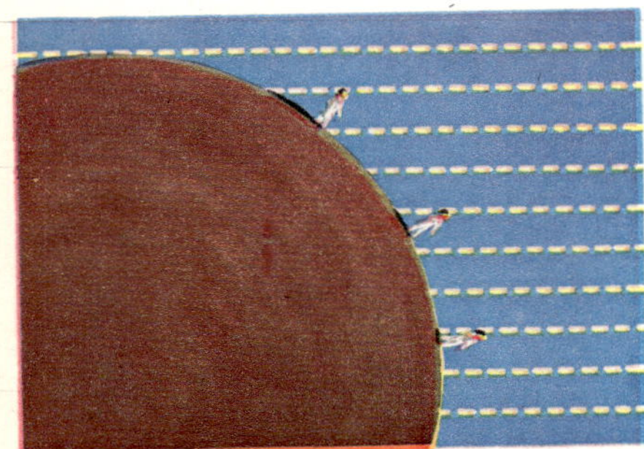

The angle of the sun's rays to the curved earth affects the length of the shadow.

By observing length of noon shadow, navigator can locate ship's position on chart.

Proof and Progress

THE EARLY GREEKS, living as they did on the coasts and islands of the Mediterranean Sea, had a taste for travel and sea-trade. It brought them wealth, as well as knowledge, from other lands. With slaves to do most of their day-to-day work, the wealthy free citizens of the Greek settlements had time on their hands to debate the affairs of the city and to argue through lengthy lawsuits.

Having mastered the new alphabet writing, they were able to leave a record of some of their arguments for all time. When travellers brought back news of what they had learned in navigation outside the Mediterranean, each announcement was a challenge to debate. Men skilled in the fashionable pastime of argument gathered around them disciples eager to study their methods.

Such a man was Pythagoras. Before 500 B.C. he founded a brotherhood of young men to whom he imparted his mathematical knowledge only after they had sworn an oath never to pass it on to an outsider. Despite this secrecy and despite the fact that he mixed magic and religion with such instruction, Pythagoras was thus a pioneer of the teaching of mathematics. A century later there were, in Athens, schools where philosophers such as Plato taught young men law, politics, public speaking and mathematics. In these new schools there were no oaths of secrecy. Teachers and pupils were free to put whatever they wished in writing for all to read.

Public study and debate led to a new way of thinking about mathematics. While the peoples of the ancient world knew many useful rules for finding areas and measuring angles, they had never attempted

Plato

Over the door of his school was written:

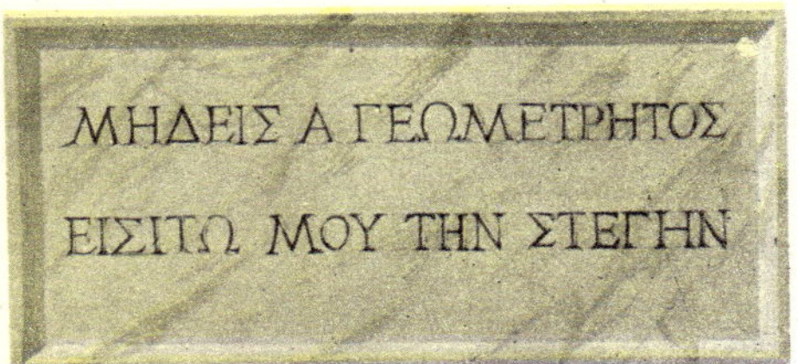
ΜΗΔΕΙΣ Α ΓΕΩΜΕΤΡΗΤΟΣ
ΕΙΣΙΤΩ ΜΟΥ ΤΗΝ ΣΤΕΓΗΝ

Let no one ignorant of geometry enter.

Sea-trading brought both wealth and knowledge to the people of the Greek islands.

to link those rules in a train of reasoning to prove that they are reliable. The argumentative Greeks insisted on putting every rule to the test of debate and answering every objection brought against it.

Long before Pythagoras, it was known that a triangle with sides 3, 4, and 5 lengths is a right-angled triangle and that the same is also true of a triangle with sides 5, 12 and 13 lengths. But Pythagoras noticed something common to both sets of numbers. If we look at the squares of the numbers in each set we see that the square of the largest number is in each case equal to the sum of the squares of the two smaller numbers:

$$3^2 = 9 \qquad 4^2 = 16 \qquad 5^2 = 25$$
$$5^2 = 25 \qquad 12^2 = 144 \qquad 13^2 = 169$$

Both these recipes for making a right-angled triangle mean that a square drawn on the longest side is equal in area to the sum of squares drawn on the two shorter sides.

Pythagoras was able to recognise the rule which embraces all such recipes. What is more interesting about him is that he asked himself two novel questions. First, is the rule *always* true? Second, is a triangle necessarily right-angled if its sides do obey this rule?

Pythagoras was not content with collecting more and more examples to show that the answer to both questions is yes for each example. He set himself the more ambitious and more useful task of proving that the answer must *always* be yes.

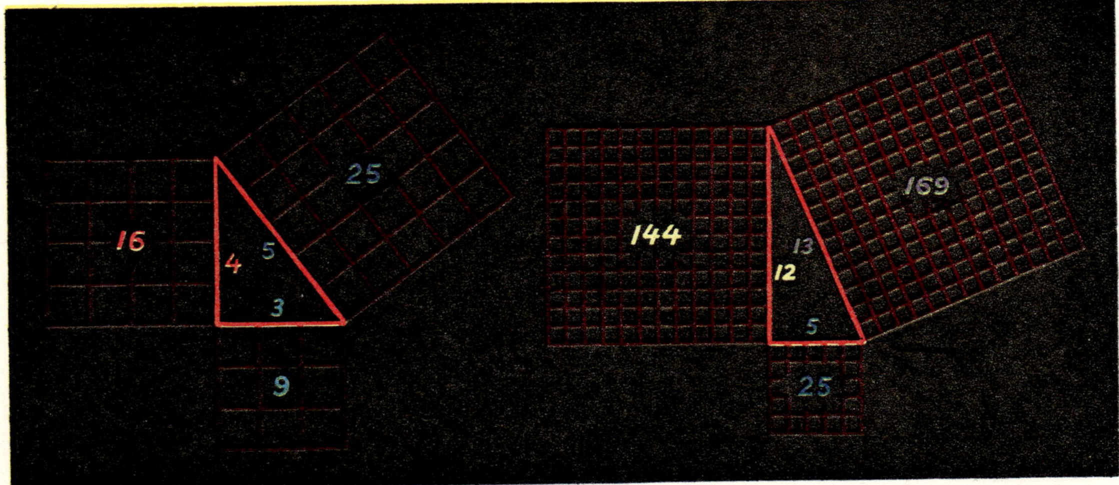

Square on longest side of a right-angled triangle equals sum of the squares on other two sides.

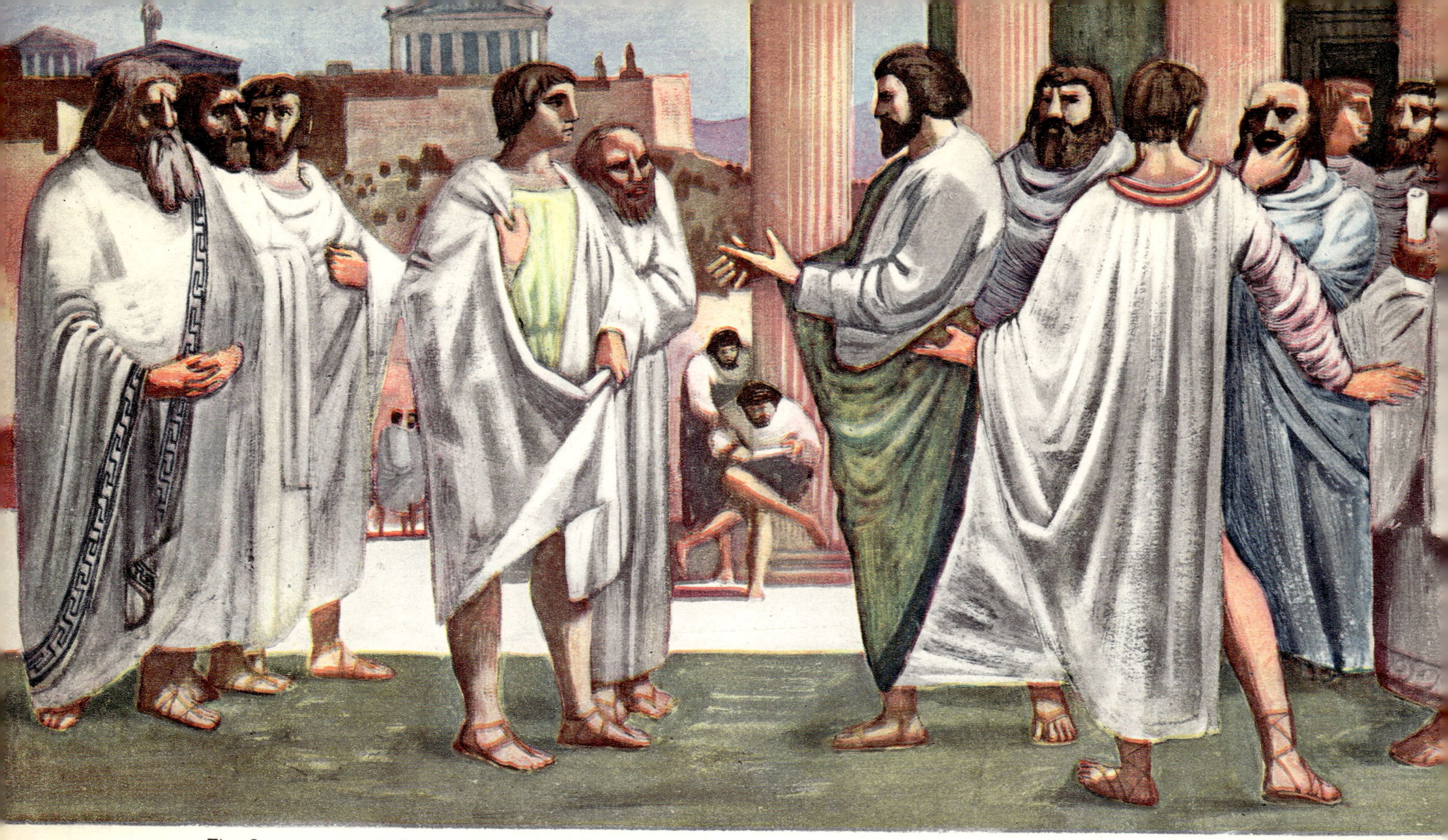

The free citizens of Greece who spent much time debating the affairs of their city-states, became expert in the art of argument.

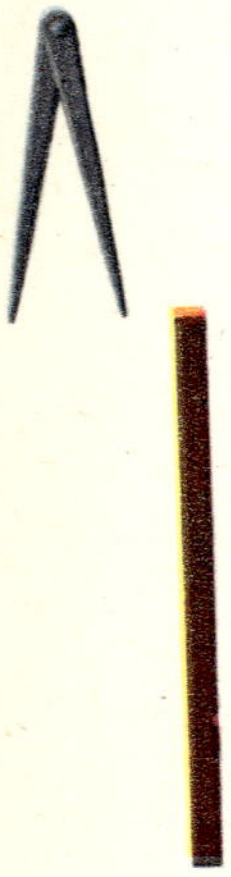

To satisfy his followers that a rule was sound, the Greek teacher of mathematics, who was also a teacher of law, would have to argue as carefully and consistently as if he were fighting a case in the courts. Just as a judge and jury want to know exactly what a lawyer means when he talks about violence or negligence, the disciples would want to know precisely what the teacher meant when he spoke of figures, lines or angles. He had to give thoroughly satisfying definitions.

Finding a form of words to satisfy everyone was not easy. It raised a host of questions. How shall we define a straight line so as to be quite sure what we are talking about? How shall we define a circle clearly enough to stop the doubter from saying that he understood us to mean any round figure, such as a sphere or an oval?

As the argument continued, it became clear that the best way of defining a particular figure, such as the triangle or the regular hexagon, is, usually, to state how you make it with the means at your disposal. This raises yet another question: what means will everyone agree to put at your disposal? The only means the Greeks agreed upon were the ruler for making a straight line and the compass for drawing a circle.

The cautious Greeks would take very little for granted. They accepted on trust only definitions and ideas that seemed quite evident. Everything else had to be proved up to the hilt; but the teacher

Problem: To draw an even six-sided figure.

Circle marked with arcs of circle size.

Cross-points joined with straight lines.

A perfect hexagon.

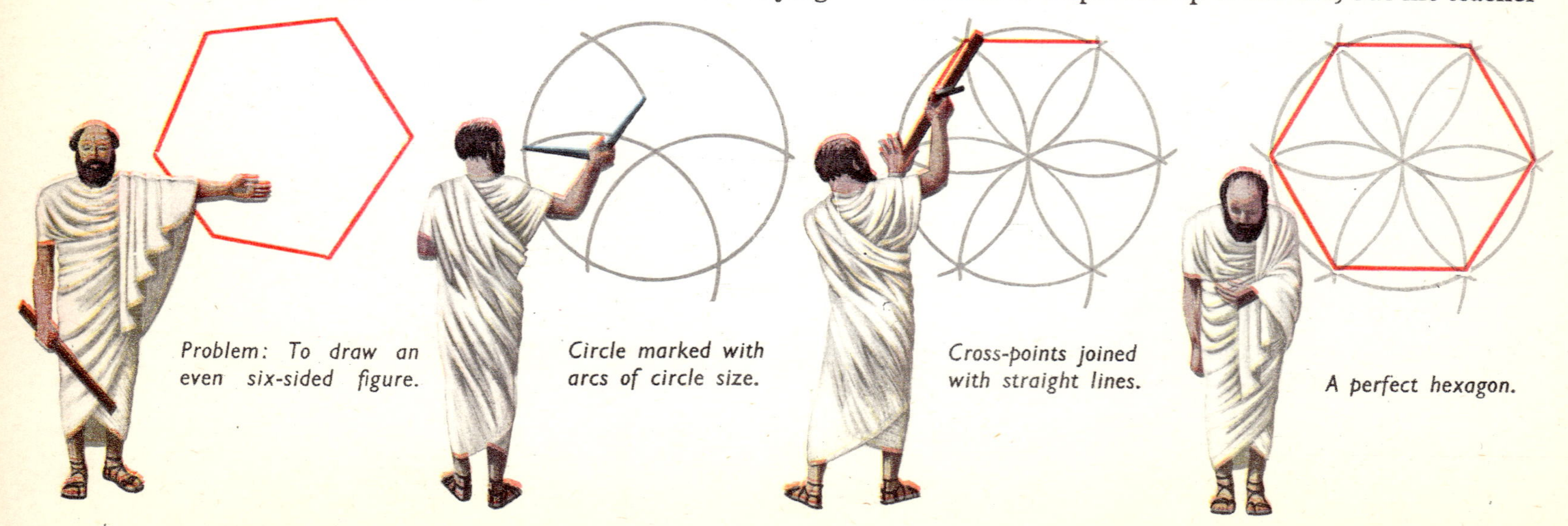

Euclid's general proof of Pythagoras's Theorem.

Euclid's work set the pattern for all that we mean by proving a case in mathematics.

In Greek . . .

In Arabic . . .

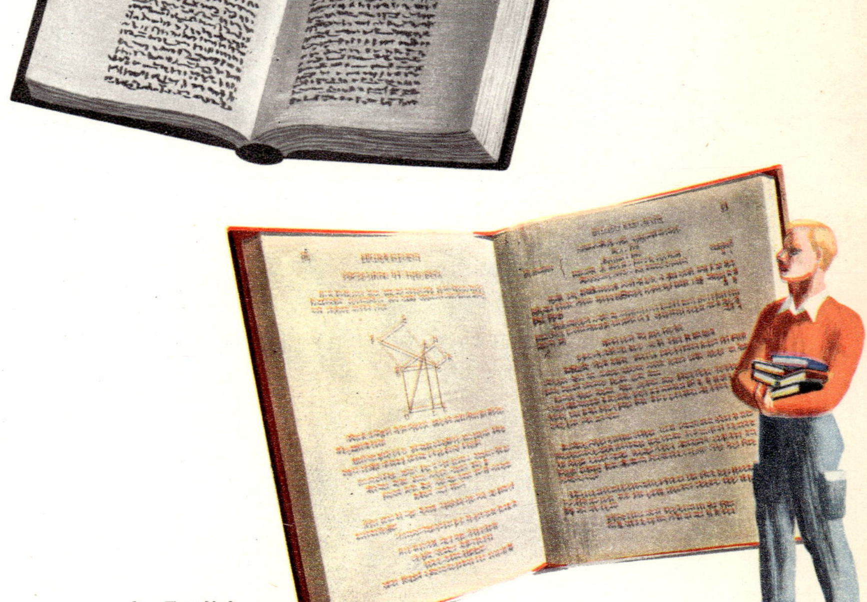

In English . . .

who had thus proved that a new rule was sound could use the same rule when proving another. There was no need to start right at the beginning again. By arranging his proofs in order, with one rule leading to the next, he could save a lot of tiresome repetition. This was the way in which the great philosopher, Plato, taught the youth of Athens in the fourth century B.C.

Before Greek times there had been no logical system of rules—no science of geometry. There had been only disconnected recipes—for making angles of various sizes and triangles of different shape, for finding the area or circumference of a circle, and so forth. By the time of Plato it was possible to shape all these into an orderly and reasonable scheme of rules.

This vast scheme has come down to us through the writings of one man, Euclid of Alexandria. About 300 B.C. Euclid wrote a series of textbooks which have proved to be the best-sellers of all time. A thousand years later, when so many Greek writings had been lost or destroyed, Euclid's *Elements* were translated into Arabic and studied in the Moslem universities. Until fifty years ago translations into modern languages were used as textbooks in European and American schools. Even today school geometry is still mainly a streamlined version of the geometry of Euclid.

We now know that Euclid took for granted some things which need not necessarily be true when we use geometry in the service of astronomy. Indeed, Euclid's geometry is now only one of several possible systems. Yet his work still remains the model of everything we mean when we talk about proving a case in mathematics.

A Greek book in Euclid's time was a bundle of papyrus scrolls.

Treasury of Cnidus shows use of triangle and parallel lines.

The Greeks studied geometry less for any practical benefits it might bring them than for fun. Yet they found that the knowledge they gained proved useful in the world's work. It was useful for building, for navigation and for astronomy, for the layout of cities and for the design of musical instruments. As the science of land measurement it especially helped the surveyor.

Among the rules which the Greeks had mastered by the time of Pythagoras are these two: (1) the three angles of any triangle add up to two right angles (180°); (2) if two angles of a triangle are equal, the sides opposite to them will also be equal. From the first rule we can see that if one angle is a right-angle (90°) and another is half a right-angle (45°), the third must also be half a right-angle (45°). From the second rule we know that the sides opposite the two angles of 45° are equal.

When sunbeams strike the earth at an angle of 45°, a pillar, its shadow and the sunbeams form just such a triangle. This gives the surveyor a method of measuring the height of the pillar without the trouble of climbing it. Pillar and shadow are both opposite an angle of 45°, so both are of equal length. Instead of measuring the height of the pillar, the surveyor can measure the shadow.

When we know the rule about a triangle of this kind, we can apply it in many other ways. For example, we can tell how far out at sea a ship is if its course lies parallel to the shore. All we have to do is to find one point where a person can sight it at exactly a right-angle, and a second point where another can sight it, at the same time, at half a right-angle. The distance between these two points is the same as the distance of the ship from the shore.

Thales, the Greek master-pilot who was at one time the teacher of the young Pythagoras, boasted that he disclosed this trick of measuring to the priests of Egypt. More likely it was the other way round; but we can be sure that the priests could not give as good reasons for believing the rule to be true as could the logically-minded Greeks.

Compass and ruler were the only tools of Greek geometry.

Tower of Greek design, built in Roman times.

Measuring height: Sun's rays are parallel, so both these triangles have the same shape. The height of the stick bears the same relationship to the length of its shadow as the height of the pyramid bears to the length of its shadow measured from the middle of the base.

Thales probably knew a second rule for finding the height of a pyramid from its shadow; and the Egyptians probably knew the same recipe without being able to prove why the rule, which is the master-rule of surveying, is always true. In any two triangles whose corresponding angles are all the same, the ratio of the lengths of any corresponding pair of sides is also the same. Thus the height of a pole will have the same ratio to the length of its noon shadow as the height of the pyramid has to the length of *its* noon shadow added to half the width of its base.

The surveyor who knew only the rule applying to a triangle with two angles of 45° could not measure the height of a pyramid from its shadow except on certain fixed days in the year when the noon sun stood at just the correct angle in the heavens. Once he had learned the rule about corresponding triangles he could do so at any season of the year.

It was not until some three hundred years after the time of Thales that the Greeks accomplished their most interesting feat of surveying. The scene, once more, was set in the Nile Valley.

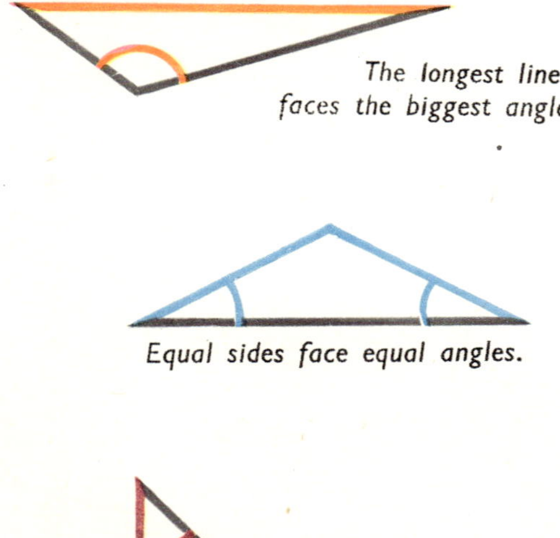

The longest line faces the biggest angle.

Equal sides face equal angles.

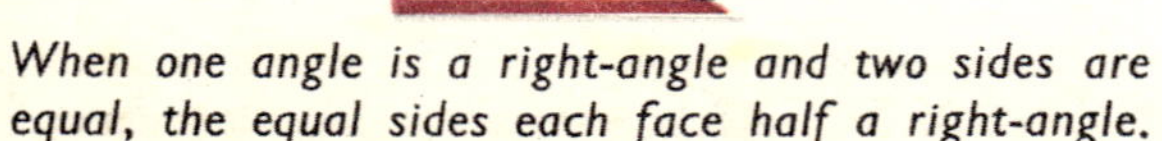

When one angle is a right-angle and two sides are equal, the equal sides each face half a right-angle.

Measuring distance: Ship is sighted at right-angle to shore and at half right-angle. Distance between sighting points is distance of ship.

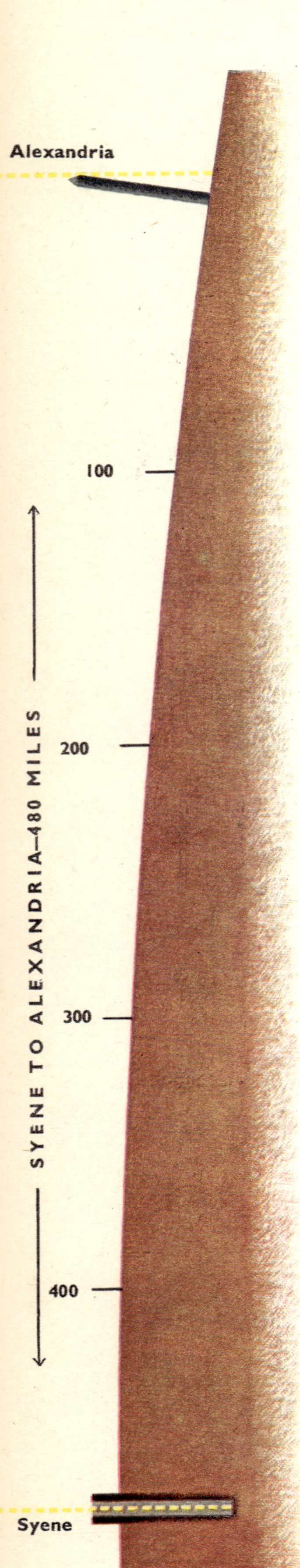

The noon sunbeam strikes Alexandria and Syene at different angles. This clue enabled Eratosthenes to measure the Earth's size.

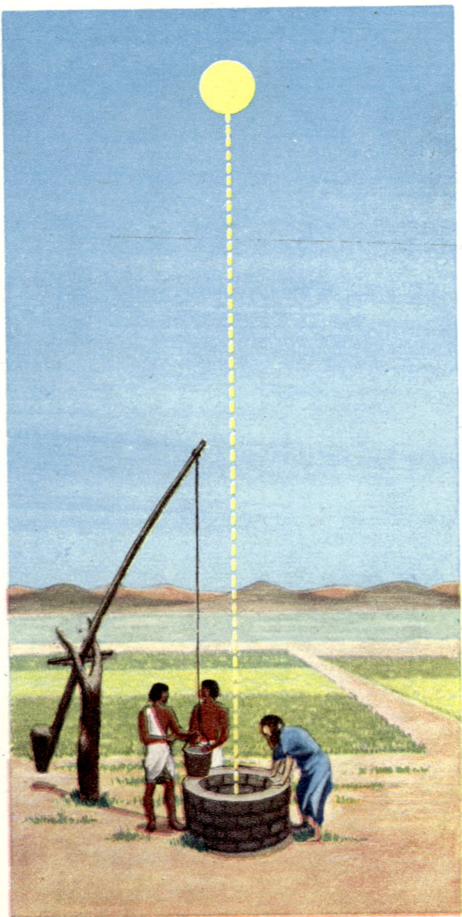

After Alexander the Great, king of what is now Greece, had conquered Egypt (332 B.C.), the city of Alexandria, built by his orders and named after him, became the chief seat of learning in the Mediterranean.

One of the many brilliant mathematicians who taught in its schools was Eratosthenes. About 240 B.C., as librarian of Alexandria's already unsurpassed library of scrolls, he learned that Syene, near what is now called Aswan, stands almost exactly on the Tropic of Cancer. At noon the reflection of the midsummer sun was there visible in the water of a deep well. This showed that the sun was directly overhead and that its beams therefore pointed in a straight line towards the middle of the earth. On the same day, measurement of the noon shadow cast by a pillar at Alexandria shows that the sunbeam strikes the earth at an angle of 7 1/5° off the vertical. We know

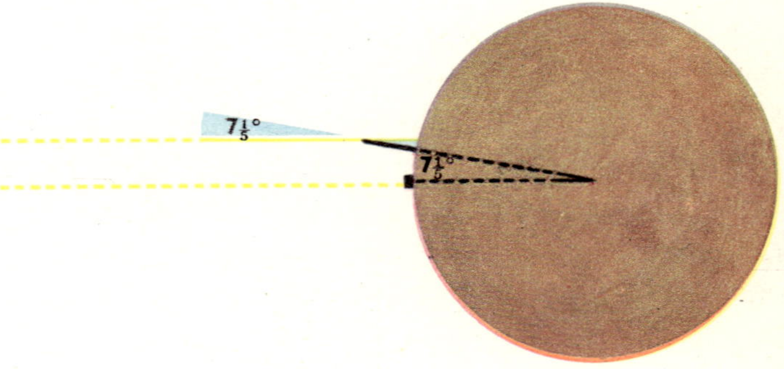

that sunbeams travel in parallel straight lines, so we may account for the difference only by the curve of the earth.

If we draw two parallel straight lines, one to show the sunbeam at Alexandria and the other to show the sunbeam at Syene, we see that the line on which the vertical pillar stands cuts through both of them. It cuts the first at the surface of the earth, and the second at the middle of the earth. The Greeks knew that when a straight line cuts across two parallel straight lines, it makes equal angles with both of them. Eratosthenes thus knew that the angle between Alexandria, the middle of the earth, and Syene must be 7 1/5°, which is exactly one-fiftieth of the 360° circle.

Syene lies nearly due south of Alexandria, and the road between them therefore lies almost exactly on a great circle passing through the North and the South Poles. Since it is almost exactly 480 miles long, the great circle is 50 times 480 miles in length. That is, the circumference of the earth is about 24,000 miles. Eratosthenes gave this remarkably accurate estimate of the size of our earth more than seventeen hundred years before Magellan's ships first sailed round it.

The Greeks of this period used mathematics in many ways we are apt to regard as modern. Archimedes, the greatest mathematician of the age, was also the inventor of many mechanical devices. He made a screw which revolved inside a tightly fitting cylinder, raising water as it turned. This was used for irrigation and for draining ships. While testing whether a crown was of pure gold or of mixed gold and silver, he discovered the principle of buoyancy. That is, a body plunged into fluid loses as much of its weight as will counterbalance the weight of the fluid it displaces. We use this principle today in making hydrometers to measure the density of liquids.

Among his many contributions to mathematics he was able to give a much more accurate value for π. We have seen that we can get a rough-and-ready value by taking the average of the boundaries or areas of the squares which just enclose and just fit inside the circle. We can cut down the possibility of error by narrowing the limits of the inside and outside figures. Our diagram shows how the limits are narrowed by using twelve-sided figures instead of squares. Archimedes went further. He used regular figures with 48 sides and was thus able to find a value which is still regarded as accurate enough for most practical purposes of design and engineering.

He also discovered how to find the volumes of various solid figures. Two of them, the sphere and the cylinder, were shown on his tombstone.

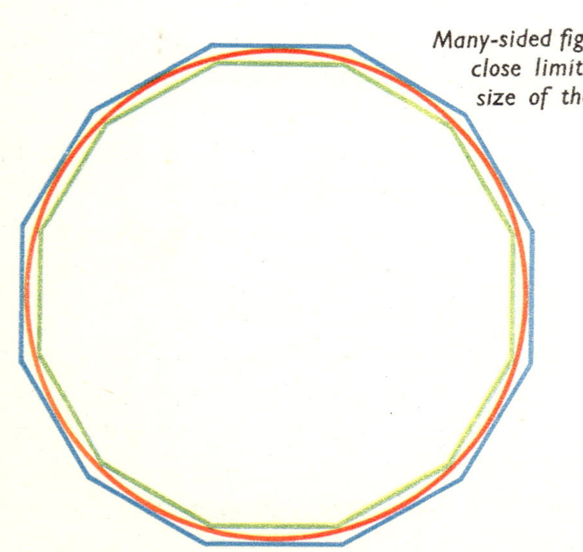

Many-sided figures set close limits to the size of the circle.

Archimedes uses water-test to check that crown is pure gold.

Archimedes' screw, revolving inside a cylinder, drains water from a ship's hold.

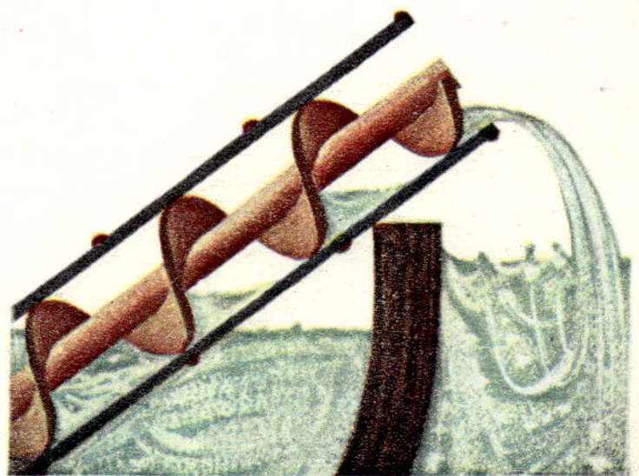

Archimedes chose two simple geometric figures to mark his tomb.

Alexandria, geometrically planned capital of Greek learning.

Strings of lengths 12, 9, 8 and 6 give notes doh, fah, soh, doh.

Hipparchus, who lived half a century after Archimedes, condensed the essentials of Greek geometry for the use of the astronomer and the surveyor in what we now call a table of sines.

We know that the angles of a triangle add up to two right-angles. If a triangle contains a right-angle and one known angle (A), the third angle, (B), must be the difference between a right-angle and A:

A
B
90

B is 90° minus A.

The ratio of the length of the side opposite A to that of the longest side is called the *sine* of A. This ratio is the same for all right-angled triangles which contain the same known angle (A). From the rule of Pythagoras, it is possible to find this ratio, or sine, when the known angle (A) is 60°, 45° or 30°. From another rule which he himself discovered, Hipparchus worked out many other sines, thus giving the surveyor or astronomer a wide range of angles with which to work.

The world of which Alexandria remained the capital of learning for seven hundred years was one which gave every encouragement to the development of arts and sciences which need the aid of mathematics. Sea-trade fostered the study of navigation and astronomy; frequent military campaigns called for more surveying and map-making; the demand for weapons of war led to a closer study of mining problems and mechanics. It is difficult to set a limit to the technical advances which might have been made if it had not been for the difficulty which the Greek world had in dealing with numbers.

The word arithmetic is a Greek word: but the Greeks did not mean by arithmetic what we ourselves mean—calculating with numerals. Perhaps it meant something closer to: getting fun out of figures. Numbers standing for the lengths of strings that would give the notes of the scale intrigued Pythagoras and his disciples. Figurate numbers, which stand for points that one can lay

In Greece music was a branch of mathematics.

ADDING ODD NUMBERS

The sum of the first two odd numbers is $2 \times 2 = 4$; the sum of the first three is $3 \times 3 = 9$; the sum of the first four is $4 \times 4 = 16$.

out in a geometrical pattern, had a special fascination. The best-known are the so-called triangular numbers, 1, 3, 6, 10, and so on, built up like this: 1, 1+2, 1+2+3, 1+2+3+4, etc. One of the sworn secrets of the Pythagorean Brotherhood was how to say what any particular number in the set is. The rule is simple: if asked to give the fifth number in the set, you multiply 5 by (5+1) and divide the result by two, which gives 15; if asked to give the twentieth number, you multiply 20 by (20+1) and divide the result by two, which gives 210.

Playing with pebbles may have given the Greeks the clue to a rule for finding the sum of consecutive odd numbers beginning with 1. If we add ten such numbers, the total is $10 \times 10 = 100$; if we add twenty, the total is $20 \times 20 = 400$.

ADDING CONSECUTIVE NUMBERS

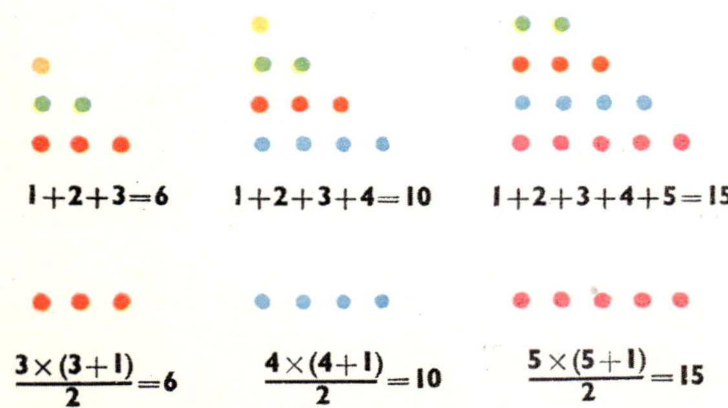

Another kind of play with numbers and ideas is well shown in a conundrum put forward by Zeno, a very wise mathematician of Alexandria. Like all his friends, he knew very well that the swiftest runner in a race will overtake his fellows; but when he brought numbers into the argument, it seemed as though Achilles could not overtake a slow-moving tortoise given a good start.

The puzzle runs something like this: Achilles runs ten times as fast as the tortoise. He gives the tortoise a start of one-tenth of a mile. While Achilles runs this tenth of a mile, the tortoise moves on another hundredth of a mile; while Achilles covers that distance the tortoise goes another thousandth of a mile; and while Achilles covers it, the tortoise goes on another ten-thousandth of a mile. To the Greeks it seemed, by this argument, that Achilles should always be a little behind the tortoise. Yet they knew he would really overtake it. Why is the argument wrong?

In numbers, the Greeks found mystery, magic and amusement.

In Egypt . . .

Mesopotamia . . .

and China, the earliest forms of writing consisted of a different picture to stand for each word.

There is no difficulty in answering the question from the practical point of view. With our own numeral system we can quite simply write the ordinary fraction 1/9 as the decimal fraction $0.\dot{1}$, in which the dot over the 1 is a short way of saying that 1 repeats itself over and over again, for ever. We thus see at once that 1/10+1/100+1/1000+1/10,000, and so on for ever, is exactly 1/9. So Achilles will overtake the tortoise exactly one-ninth of a mile from his starting point. "For ever" does not mislead us. Our own number signs tell us we inevitably reach a limit however long we go on piling up such smaller and smaller fractions.

Strangely enough, the alphabet, which helped them in so many other ways, hindered the Greeks in the art of calculating.

The early priests of Egypt and Mesopotamia used pictures to stand for words or ideas. The man who wanted to read their inscriptions had to memorise thousands of separate picture signs. The Greeks, who inherited alphabetic writing, had only to master the shapes of a few letters and to memorise the sounds they represent. They hoped that the alphabet which so simplified word-language would also simplify number-language. So they began to use letters to stand for numbers.

At first they used the initial letters of words, just as we might use T for ten and H for hundred. The early Greek words for ten, hundred and thousand were deka (Δεκα), hekto (Hεκτο) and kilo (Χιλο), and they provided the number signs Δ for 10, H for 100, X for 1,000. To make up large numbers, the writer repeated these signs as needed. Apart from the fact that the early Greeks used new signs for 5, 50 and 500, their number script was much like that of Egypt. We can see this when we write the same number (3420) in both scripts.

𓆼𓆼𓆼 𓍢𓍢𓍢𓍢 𓎆𓎆

X X X H H H H Δ Δ

The later Greeks developed an entirely different style. They used the first nine letters of the alphabet to stand for the numbers 1 to 9, the next

Alphabetic writing, as on the Hebrew coins, began among the Jews and Phoenicians, and was later adapted and used by the Greeks.

Hebrew Coins

Greek Plaque

The name inscribed on this Greek tomb is Democleides Demetrio.

Learning to spell: the word is the same as our flower-name, IRIS.

nine letters for 10 to 90, and the last nine for 100 to 900. They made any number a thousand times as large as its normal value simply by placing a stroke in front of it. The only advantage of this system was that large numbers took up less space. Thus 3420 was written as /ΓΥΚ. To offset this trifling convenience, however, the later Greek number-system made calculation more difficult. When an Egyptian priest wrote ℮℮℮ ∩∩ ||| (323) he could easily see that it meant three beads in the hundreds column of his abacus, two in the tens column, three in the units column. When a Greek wrote ΤΚΓ (323) it told him nothing about how to lay out his abacus.

While the world was saddled with Greek number signs, there could be no simple table of multiplication such as we now learn when very young. The mathematicians of Alexandria did have scrolls of some tables to avoid doing all their calculations on the counting-frame, but a scroll would need to be almost endless to hold all the numbers we need to multiply in modern astronomy.

Today we use letters as a kind of shorthand in mathematics. Instead of saying that the area of a triangle is equal to its base multiplied by its height and divided by two, we say it is $\frac{bh}{2}$. But for the Greeks, who used every letter of the alphabet to stand for a different number, such a shorthand was almost impossible.

The Romans, who succeeded the Greeks as masters of the Mediterranean world, patterned their number-system on that of the early Greeks. We rightly think of the Romans as a nation of conquerors, but they were never able to conquer the art of calculating as we know it today. Even simple multiplication was a slow and space-consuming process. The Roman merchant might use numerals for recording, but calculating was still a task for the slave working with an abacus.

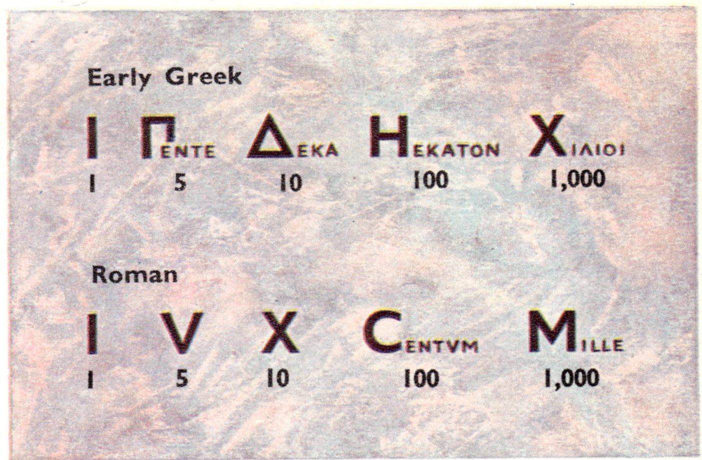

Roman numerals followed the pattern set by the early Greeks.

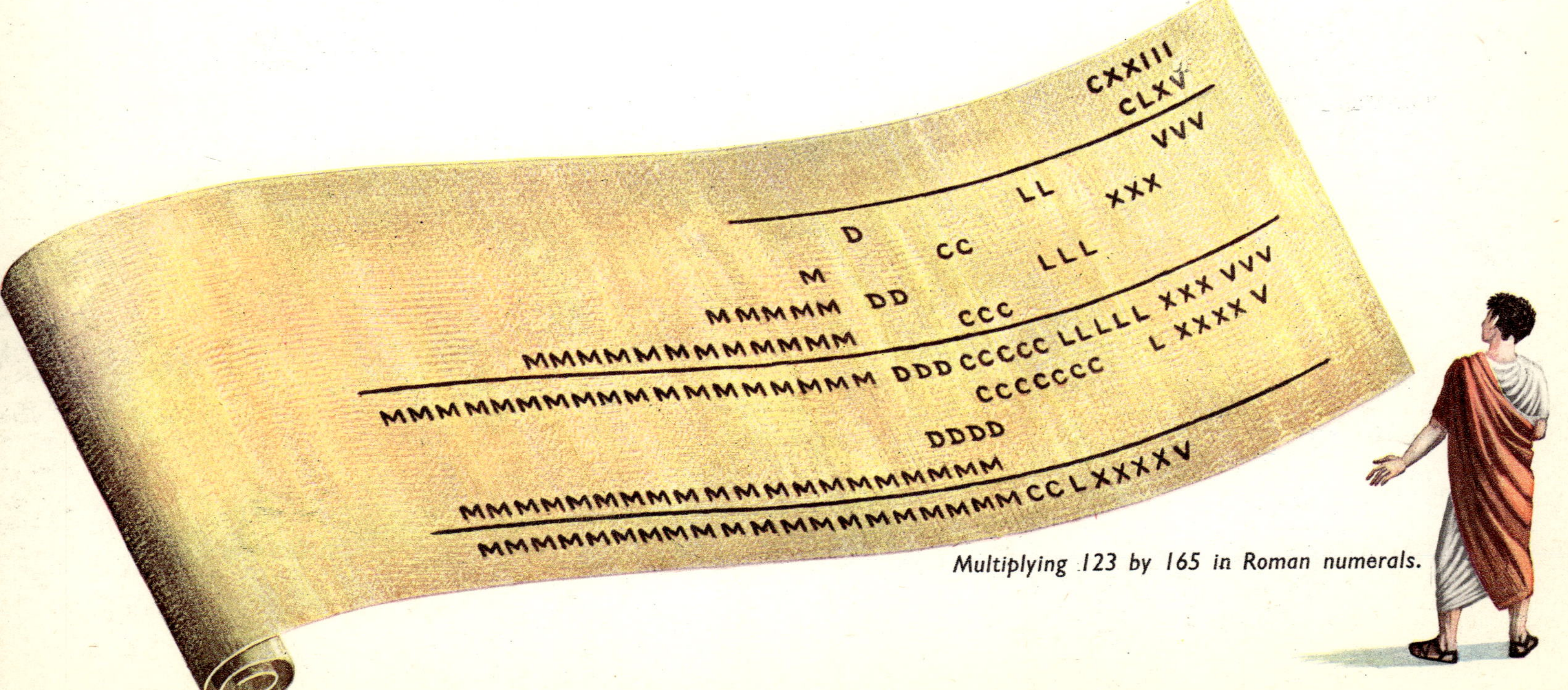

Multiplying 123 by 165 in Roman numerals.

Wherever the conquering Roman legions went, they brought law and order and left a legacy of fine roads, buildings and bridges.

About two thousand years ago, the Roman legions conquered the whole of southern Europe, all Gaul, most of Britain, the northern fringe of Africa and a large area of west Asia. Throughout the conquered regions they built a vast network of good roads and fine bridges. They built also a new system of law and government. Yet the Greek language long remained the language of learning.

In the fourth century A.D., the Empire was divided into two parts; the western half with its capital at Rome and the eastern with its capital at Constantinople, now Istanbul. By then the Empire was under strong pressure from the revolt of non-Roman troops inside its borders and from powerful tribes warring on its frontiers. Gradually the west lost contact with the Eastern Empire which still preserved the language and tradition of Greek learning.

When the mighty Roman Empire decayed, a small remnant of the eastern half, embracing Greece and the country a little north of it, remained intact, keeping a little of its old glory. Meanwhile the west soon forgot utterly the language and science of Greece. What learning remained there was preserved by monks who brought the art of writing to Gaul and Britain.

CAESAR

DE BELLO GALLICO

LIBER PRIMUS.

1. GALLIA est omnis divisa in partes tres, quarum 1
unam incolunt Belgae, aliam Aquitani, tertiam qui ipsorum lingua Celtae, nostra Galli appellantur. Hi omnes lingua, in- 2
stitutis, legibus inter se differunt. Gallos ab Aquitanis Garumna flumen, a Belgis Matrona et Sequana dividit. Horum omnium fortissimi sunt 3
Belgae, propter[...] cultu atque humanitate provinciae [...]nimeque ad eos merc[...]

Gaul is divided into three parts, viz. Belgium, Gaul proper, and Aquitania.

Roman numerals, Roman engineering and the Latin language have remained part of our western heritage to the present day.

Because Western Europe learned its letters from monks of the Roman Church, Latin, the language of the Church service, there became the language of learning. Even in the time of Columbus books about divinity, law and medicine were mostly in Latin. The only numerals used were Roman numerals which label each groove of the abacus differently, as M, C, X, I. Today we still see traces of this long Latin influence. We still label our books as Vol. I and Vol. II; and the dials of our clocks often carry Roman numerals.

Before the West could make any real progress in the art of calculation and in science, it had to have help. Help came from the East.

A Roman aqueduct in Turkey.

Numbers and Nothing

ONE OF THE world's oldest civilisations grew up in the valley of the River Indus, in India. Like those of the Nile and the Euphrates, it learned its first lessons in mathematics through astronomy, the gateway to time-reckoning and to temple-building. Several centuries before Rome rose to power, the mathematicians of India had found a close value for π. In the arithmetic of trade, the merchants of India were the equals of those of Mesopotamia.

Until about two thousand years ago, they probably used numerals made up of horizontal strokes. But when they began to use dried palm leaves as writing material and developed a flowing style of writing, they also began to join up these strokes, so that = became ᘔ and ≡ became ⋧ . In this way they gradually built up different signs for each number up to nine. Each sign could conveniently be used to indicate the number of pebbles in *any* groove of the abacus.

Had progress stopped short there, it would not have amounted to much. If ᘔᘔ merely stands for two pebbles in any two grooves, it can have many different meanings, such as twenty-two, two hundred and two, two thousand and twenty, and so on. We need to be told not only how many pebbles in a groove, but also which groove they are in.

Somewhere in India, some unknown person, probably a counting-house clerk, hit on a device which does this for us. He used the figure on the extreme right to stand for pebbles in the units groove, the next figure to the left to stand for pebbles in the tens groove, and so on. To indicate an empty column, he used a dot, just as we now use a zero. Thus ᘔᘔ could mean only 22. ᘔ.ᘔ. could mean only 2020.

With this system, we no longer rely on space-consuming repetition; and we can record the same number on any groove of the abacus by using the same sign. But saving space is only a small advantage, as the later Greeks must have learned. The great advantage of the Hindu system is that it enables us to *calculate* with numerals.

The ancient systems of writing – Egyptian, Babylonian, Greek, Roman and Chinese – all relied on the use of different symbols for the same number of pebbles in different grooves of the abacus. Before you could do written or mental calculations with them, you would therefore need to learn a different table of addition and of multiplication for each groove. When you have only nine different signs, each of which can show the number of pebbles in any groove, and a zero to indicate empty grooves, you need learn only one simple table, once and for all. You can carry over in your head because there is only one simple table to remember. The Hindu number-language quickly led to a revolution in the art of calculation. The mathematicians of India began to think of fractions and to write them in the way that we do. By 500 A.D. India had produced mathematicians who solved problems which had baffled the greatest scholars of antiquity. The mathematician, Varahamihira, was able to calculate how to forecast the positions of planets; Aryabhata stated a rule for finding square roots and gave a value for π which is still good enough for most purposes today – 3.1416.

By about 800 A.D., Indian traders, following the age-old caravan route which passed through Persia into Mesopotamia, brought news of the new numerals to Baghdad which was then rapidly becoming the world's greatest city of learning.

New numerals stand for number of beads in any column.

0 stands for empty column.

Palm-leaf manuscripts.

As caravans of Hindu traders moved westward along the age-old trade routes, they carried not only merchandise but also ideas.

To Baghdad, magnificent capital city of the great Moslem Empire, came Hindu merchants with their wonderful new numeral system.

Early in the seventh century, Mahommed, founder and prophet of the Moslem religion, united the whole of Arabia under his leadership. For more than three centuries after his death, his followers carried the new religion across the whole of North Africa, into Spain and Portugal, and eastward through Asia beyond the River Indus.

About 762 they founded the city of Baghdad and made it the seat of government of a rapidly-growing empire. About forty years later, under the Caliph, Harun ar-Rashid, it became the capital of learning of the western world, just as Alexandria had been during Greek and Roman times.

In learning, Baghdad made the best of both worlds, East and West. Merchants and mathematicians from the East brought with them the new number signs and the arithmetic of India. Heretics, who had fled from the West, brought copies of scientific works written while Alexandria was still at its prime. These included treatises on astronomy and geography and Euclid's geometry. By order of the Caliph, Moslem scholars translated such works into Arabic, the language of their sacred book, the Koran. Thus, the science and geometry of Greece became available throughout the Moslem world, now equipped with an arithmetic far better than the best the Greeks had known.

To this growing body of knowledge the East made two other contributions. Chinese prisoners, captured during a skirmish on the frontier, taught

Chinese brought paper-making.

Persians brought astrology.

Baghdad the art of paper-making, while Persian astrologers, who added a spice of eastern magic to a sound knowledge of the heavens, gave the Caliph's court a keen interest in astronomy.

In observatories built by command of the Caliph, astronomers advanced the science of map-making far beyond the level it had reached in Alexandria. In the schools of Baghdad trigonometry flourished. Because they had mastered the new arithmetic of India, Moslem mathematicians could make much fuller use of the geometry of Euclid and of Archimedes. The astronomer equipped the mariner with nautical almanacs for navigation by sun and stars and gave him improved instruments, designed in the observatories. The geographer had new and better tools for land-survey.

Never before in history had knowledge advanced in a single century as it did between 800 and 900 A.D., where East met West in Baghdad.

Refugees from the west brought Greek geometry into Baghdad.

Arabian astrolabe of eleventh century.

In elaborate new observatories, Arab astronomers accumulated an ever-increasing knowledge of the movements of the heavenly bodies.

How various kinds of knowledge mingled in Baghdad and slowly penetrated into Europe.

Our map shows how the new learning swept across the western world. The drawings near the orange arrows show what kinds of knowledge met and mingled in Baghdad. Pale green areas show where the conquering Moslems carried knowledge with them. Red arrows show the routes along which learning spread beyond the Moslem Empire.

By the year 1000 A.D., the greater part of the old Roman Empire had come under Moslem rule. Spain, now occupied by Moorish followers of Mohammed, especially enjoyed the benefits of the new learning. In its Moslem universities, students could study the geometry of Greece, the arithmetic of India, and the sciences of astronomy, of trigonometry and of geography which the scholars of Baghdad had done so much to advance.

Early in the twelfth century a Christian monk, Adelard of Bath, disguised himself as a Moslem and studied for many years at the University of Cordova. There he made translations of the works of Euclid and of the Moslem mathematician, Alkarismi. These he smuggled back to Britain.

During the following century, Jewish physicians, trained in Spanish universities, carried the new learning to France and to Italy, founding medical schools in Christian universities which had formerly ignored the teaching of science. Moslem culture also reached Europe along the sea-lanes from Sicily and by the routes crusaders followed when returning from the Holy Land.

By 1400 A.D. the merchants of Italy, France, Germany and Britain were using the new numerals, and schools for the teaching of the new arithmetic began to spring up throughout Europe. Half a century later, when printing began, textbooks of arithmetic and nautical almanacs were among the chief products of the printing press.

In 15th-century Portugal, the sailor prince, Henry the Navigator, set up a school where Jewish teachers, trained in the universities of Spain, instructed pilots in navigation. The success of Columbus is in no small measure due to the pilots he enlisted: Jewish experts trained in Moslem astronomy and Moslem mathematics.

HINDU, 800 A.D.

ARABIC, 900 A.D. ONWARDS

SPANISH, 1000 A.D.

ITALIAN, 1400 A.D.

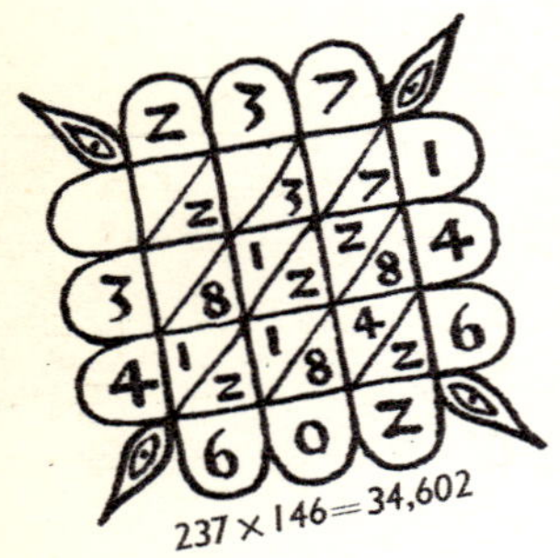
237 × 146 = 34,602

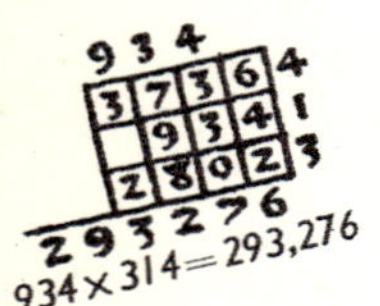
934 × 314 = 293,276

Multiplication table

From drawing in a 15th-century arithmetic.

As the new numerals passed from one land to another, they frequently changed their shape, but they always kept to the pattern of nine number-signs and a zero. It would be wrong to imagine, however, that they were immediately and everywhere acceptable. In the thirteenth century a law forbade the bankers of Florence to use them, and a hundred years later the University of Padua insisted that price-lists of books should appear in Roman numerals. But by the fifteenth century, Hindu numerals were in general use for navigation and commerce throughout Western Europe. For centuries after that many people still used the abacus and counting board, but more and more were eager to learn the new arithmetic.

Textbooks which poured from the early printing-presses spread far afield convenient ways of writing down tables and of setting out problems in addition, subtraction, multiplication and division. Many of these methods, like those shown on this page, are now interesting only as museum pieces. Much more important is the fact that the early textbooks introduced new shorthand signs into arithmetic, such as + and −. These were not deliberate mathematical inventions. It is probable that they were originally warehouse signs, used to indicate which packages were overweight, which underweight. As these early signs proved their usefulness, others were gradually introduced: × (multiply), ÷ (divide), ∴ (therefore), = (equals).

Long before modern numerals reached Christian Europe, Hindu and Moslem mathematicians had

Arithmetic may have borrowed the signs + and − from the merchants' marks for overweight and underweight.

discovered many tricks for solving number problems of the kind we now deal with by algebra. In fact, algebra is an Arabic word, but it would be a mistake to think that the Moslem mathematicians taught algebra as we now learn it. Although they no longer used letters to stand for numbers, they had never hit on the idea of using them to state a rule or problem involving numbers in a short, snappy way. The only shorthand sign they used was $\sqrt{}$ for square root.

It was not until about 1600 that algebra, as we know it, had gradually taken shape. We can see how the new system developed by working out a simple problem: if the result of multiplying a number by two and dividing the product by three is forty, what is the number? The Hindu and Moslem mathematicians might explain the solution in some such words as these: Since two-thirds of the number is forty, one-third of it is half forty, which is twenty; and the number itself is three times this, which is sixty.

An early arithmetic might have put it this way: Find the number, if $(2 \times \text{number}) \div 3 = 40$. The solution would be written something like this:

$$\frac{2 \times \text{num.}}{3} = 40\,;\ \frac{\text{num.}}{3} = \tfrac{1}{2}(40) = 20\,;\ \text{num.} = 3 \times 20 = 60$$

In modern algebra we would shorten the word number to n, drop the sign $\times$, and write the solution in simple orderly steps, as shown below.

The Moslem teacher of 1200 A.D. could certainly have given a rule for solving any problem of this sort, but he would have given it in a long, cumbersome way, like this: If you know what the answer is when you multiply any number by a second and divide it by a third, you can find the number itself by multiplying the answer by the third and dividing the result by the second.

Bead-calculation was used long after written arithmetic began.

Today we would write this more snappily by putting n for any number, s for the second, t for the third, and a for the answer. The rule then becomes much easier to remember:

$$\text{If } \frac{sn}{t} = a, \qquad n = \frac{ta}{s}$$

With new numerals, a new arithmetic and the beginnings of the new algebra, Europe was in a good position to tackle the practical problems that faced it in the Age of Discovery, soon to begin.

In the new schools of Europe, men worked to improve methods of calculation.

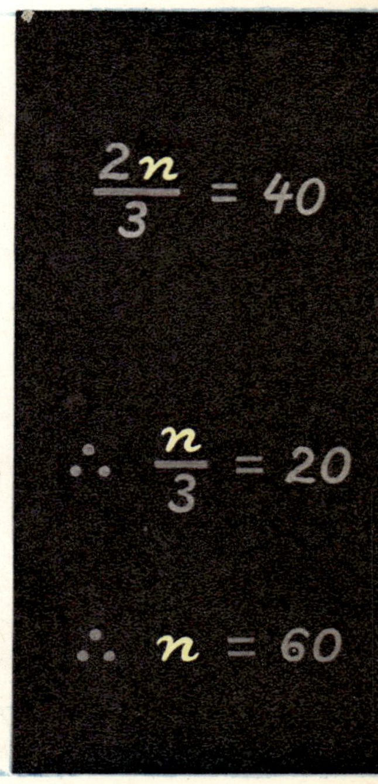

From words to the shorthand of algebra.

Graphs and Gravity

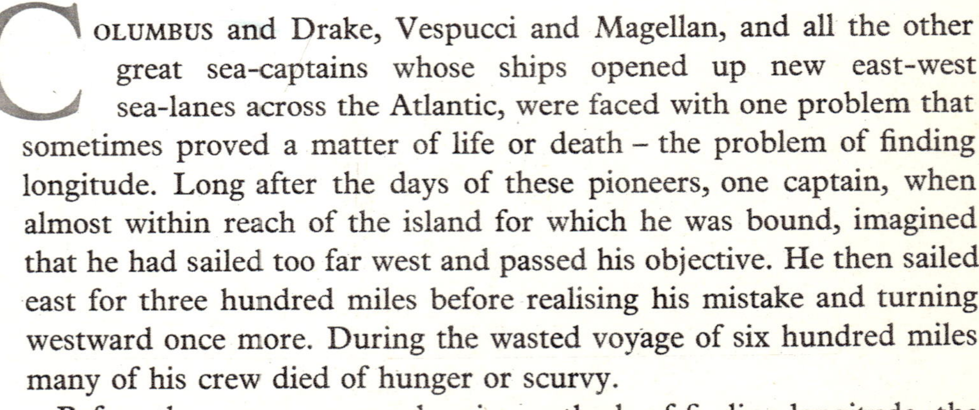

COLUMBUS and Drake, Vespucci and Magellan, and all the other great sea-captains whose ships opened up new east-west sea-lanes across the Atlantic, were faced with one problem that sometimes proved a matter of life or death – the problem of finding longitude. Long after the days of these pioneers, one captain, when almost within reach of the island for which he was bound, imagined that he had sailed too far west and passed his objective. He then sailed east for three hundred miles before realising his mistake and turning westward once more. During the wasted voyage of six hundred miles many of his crew died of hunger or scurvy.

Before there were new and easier methods of finding longitude, the explorer-mariner had no means of locating the positions of ports accurately on his map. To fix your longitude, you need to know the time where you are and to compare it with the time at some other fixed point. By comparing the times when eclipses of the moon were visible at different places, the geographer Ptolemy of Alexandria was able to fix, roughly, the longitude of some half-dozen places. Moslem astronomers and geographers knew the longitude of perhaps a score of towns. This was a great gain; but the captain of an ocean-going ship needs a way of fixing the longitude of any place at any time, and for this he must have dependable and accurate time-keeping instruments.

To early time-keepers, the Middle Ages added only crude clocks.

A swinging altar-lamp gave a clue to the law of the pendulum.

In the Age of Discovery, with ships crossing the world, men therefore needed to measure minutes and seconds accurately. For this purpose crude weight-driven clocks such as churches and monasteries had installed during the four previous centuries were of no more use than the candle-clocks, the sun-dials and the hour-glasses on which the ancient world depended.

The first clue to accurate measurement of small intervals of time was discovered in 1583, when Galileo, a young Italian medical student, watched a lamp swinging to and fro in Pisa Cathedral. Timing its motion by the beat of his pulse, Galileo found that all swings, whether wide or narrow, took the same time.

Later on, when Galileo gave up the study of medicine to take up mathematics and physics, he used a home-made water-clock to check the accuracy of this observation. While a pendulum was swinging, he allowed water to flow from a hole at the bottom of a large vessel and fall into a small one below it. If the weight of water that escaped during two separate swings was the same, he knew that both had taken an equal time.

His experiments showed that the time of swing depends only on the length of the pendulum. To double the time of swing you must make your pendulum four times as long; to treble the time of swing you must make your pendulum nine times as long. The length of the pendulum varies in the same ratio as the square of the time of swing. We now know that this rule, while correct for narrow swings, is not quite accurate when the pendulum swings through a very wide arc. In 1657 the Dutch scientist, Huygens, made use of Galileo's discovery to produce accurate pendulum-regulated clocks.

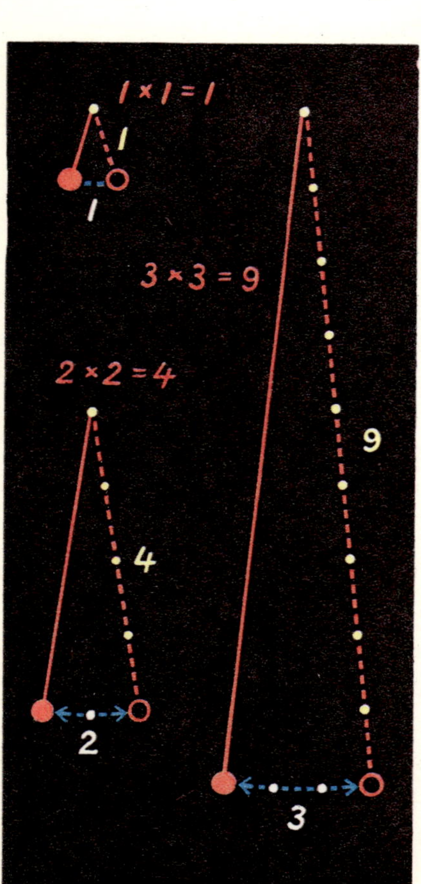

Red lines show length, blue show time. Length determines the time of swing.

Early pendulum clock.

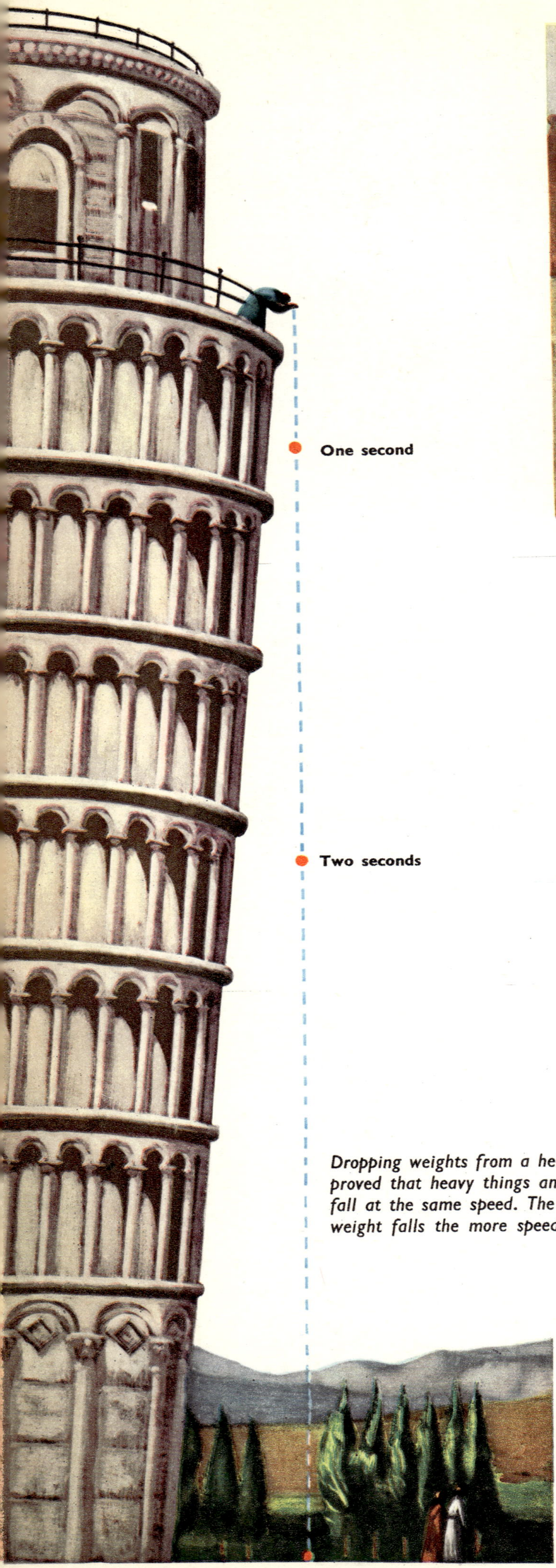

As a ball rolled down a slope, Galileo measured its acceleration with a water-device.

Before Galileo's time, people believed that the heavier an object was, the faster it would fall. Galileo's pendulum experiments, however, disproved this. For he found that the weight of the bob at the bottom of the pendulum has no effect on the time of swing. To settle the matter beyond dispute, he dropped two different weights simultaneously from the Leaning Tower of Pisa. Both the heavy one and the light one hit the ground at the same instant.

Galileo recognised that both weights increased their speed, or accelerated, as they fell. In his day there were no stop-watches for split-second timing. So he found it impossible to measure the acceleration directly. He realised, however, that gravity acts on a ball rolling down a slope just as it acts on a falling weight; but the slope itself then slows down the speed of the ball. He therefore

One second

Two seconds

Dropping weights from a height, Galileo proved that heavy things and light ones fall at the same speed. The farther any weight falls the more speed it gathers.

Three seconds

Sixteenth-century effort to apply mathematics to range-finding.

The cannon completely revolutionised warfare. Once-impregnable forts, high up on hilltops, made easy targets for the new weapon.

rolled a ball down a sloping board and timed it as he had timed the swing of the pendulum.

He found that in two seconds the ball rolls four times as far as in one second; in three seconds it rolls nine times as far as in one second. The distance it rolls varies in the same ratio as the square of the time it rolls.

This discovery makes it possible to work out the kind of path a cannon-ball follows as it hurtles through the air. At the instant it leaves the mouth of the cannon, it would move in a straight line pointing in the same direction as the gun-barrel, if there were no force of gravity to pull it downwards at a uniformly increasing rate. But because of the pull of gravity, it travels along the kind of curve which we call a parabola.

Before the time of Galileo, mathematicians had tried, without much success, to advise the artilleryman about how to decide the correct elevation for the cannon when he knew the distance of the target. When it was possible to understand how gravity affects the flight of the cannon-ball, it was also possible to work out tables of elevation, based on the distance of the target. This distance, together with the speed of the ball, decides how long the ball will be in flight and hence how long the force of gravity will be acting on it.

In the seventeenth century, military engineers trained in mathematics designed new fortifications to withstand attack by cannon. Low-built forts protected by earthworks replaced hillside fortresses which enabled the defenders of earlier times to fire down on their attackers. The new ones confronted the attackers with a more difficult target, while the defenders, with cannons placed low, could answer their fire as effectively as from a height.

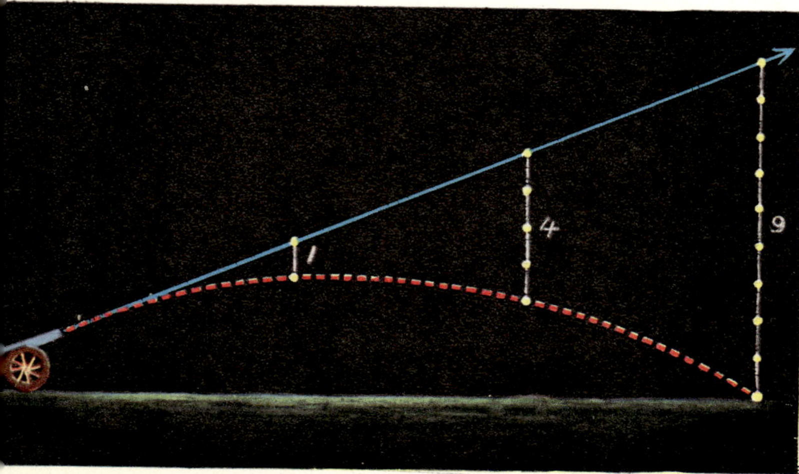

Shot falling faster and faster from course, travels in a curve.

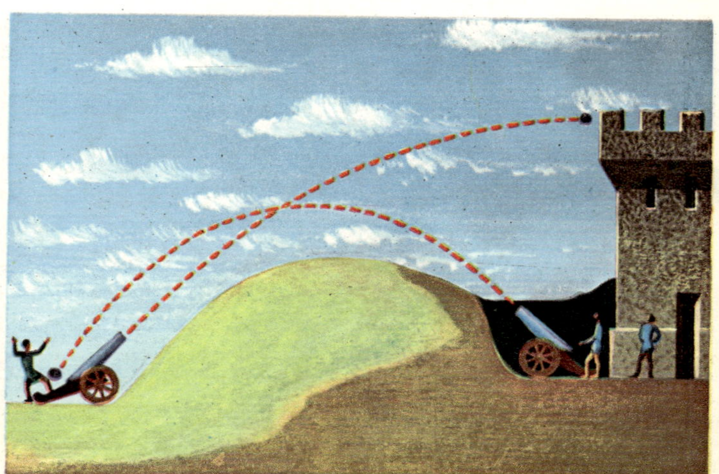

Knowledge of cannon-ball's path changed system of fortification.

The problem of finding longitude also ties up with the movement of a ball: the great ball we call our Earth. Each day the earth makes one complete spin round on its axis, from west to east. All the time, part of it is turning out of the sunlight into the shadow and part is turning out of the shadow into the sunlight. When it is noon at any given place, it is later than noon to the east and earlier than noon to the west.

Geographers divide the earth into 360° of longitude (180° for the eastern hemisphere and 180° for the western). Since there are 24 hours, or 1,440 minutes, in a day, the difference in time for each degree is 4 minutes (1440 ÷ 360). So, if we know our local time and the time at some other place at any particular moment, we can work out the difference in longitude. If it is 12 noon in London and 7 a.m. where we are standing, our local time is 300 minutes earlier than that of London; we are therefore 300 ÷ 4, or 75°, west of London – roughly the longitude of New York.

Columbus threw wood or barrel overboard from bow.

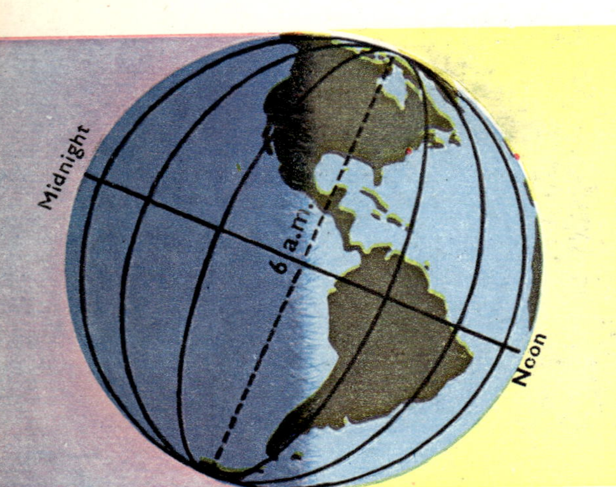

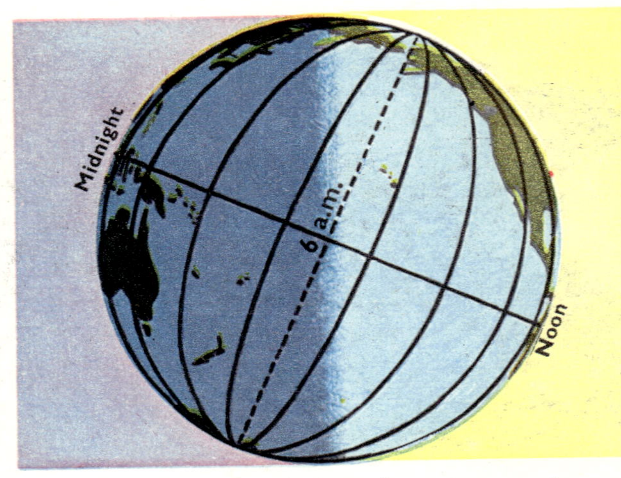

A sextant.

As the earth spins round on its axis, time moves on evenly everywhere. If, at any particular moment, a seaman knows his local time and the time at any other fixed point, he can find his longitude.

In the age of Columbus, a ship's captain could make a very close approximation to his correct local time with the help of an astrolabe, but he had no convenient method of finding the time at another fixed point. For this, he would rely on his almanac, which told him the time at which an eclipse of the moon or the disappearance of a planet behind the moon's disc might be visible at his home port. He had then to wait until he saw such an occurrence, to take his local time at that moment, and to compare it with the time shown in the almanac. His almanac would always give him the home-time of an eclipse of the moon or the home-time at which the moon would "occult"

Almanac gave the time of an eclipse at home port.

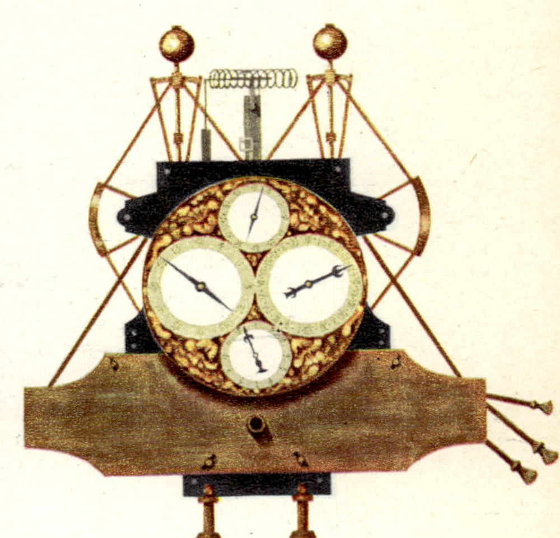

Harrison's first chronometer

The time his ship took to pass it gave him his speed. His compass gave his approximate direction.

a planet, or hide it from view; but eclipses of the moon and occultations by planets do not occur often in the course of a year.

Between times, captains had to experiment with their own ways of keeping check on their whereabouts. Having set his direction in a rough and ready way from the compass, Columbus used to throw a piece of wood or a barrel overboard from the bows. If his 50-foot ship took ten seconds to pass it, he knew he was travelling at 300 feet a minute, or roughly three-and-a-half miles an hour.

The longitude problem was solved completely only after the middle of the eighteenth century, when ships were first fitted with sextants and chronometers. The sextant gave the navigator a more accurate means of finding local time, and the chronometer enabled him to carry the time of his home port wherever he went. The first chronometer, i.e. a clock which keeps accurate time over a long sea-voyage, was invented by a self-taught English carpenter, John Harrison, at the time when Benjamin Franklin was making his great discoveries about electricity.

A century later, all sea-faring nations agreed to set their chronometers by Greenwich standard time and to measure longitude from the line on which Greenwich Observatory, London, stands.

Astrolabe gave local time.

Greenwich Observatory about 1700

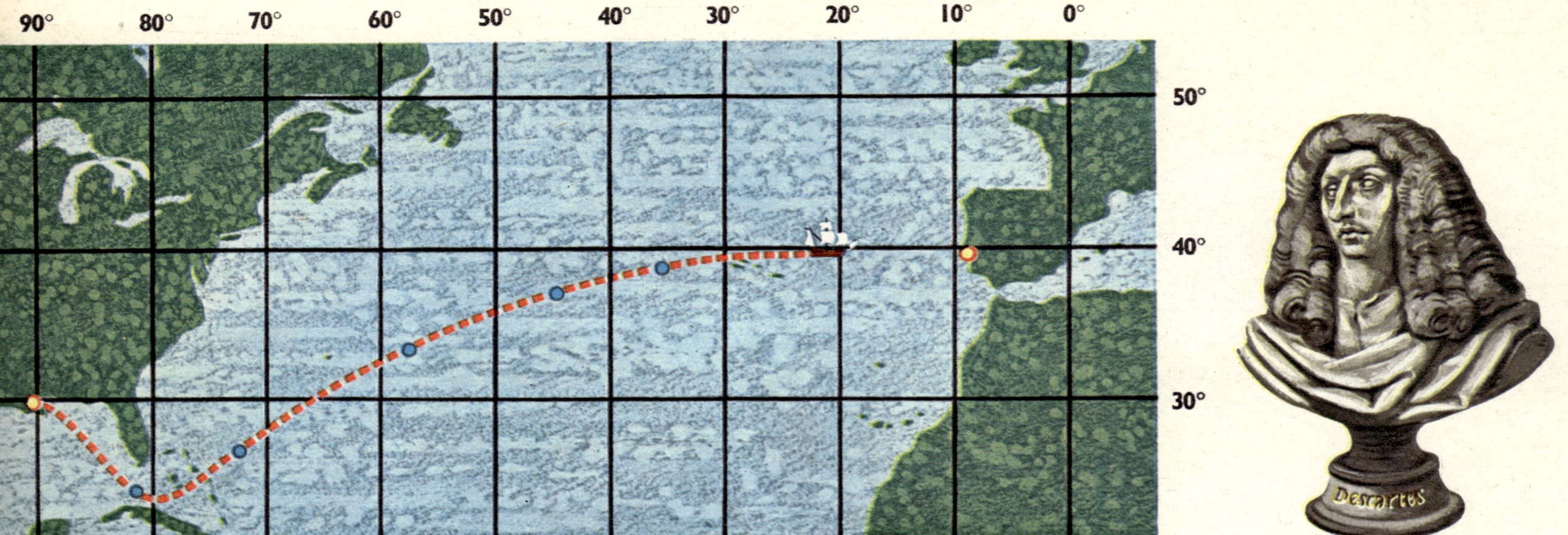

On a map marked with lines of latitude and longitude, one curve can sum up a ship's voyage.

During the sixteenth and seventeenth centuries, navigators began to plot the day-to-day position of their ships on maps marked with lines of latitude and longitude. A connecting line drawn through all these points gave the navigator a convenient summary of the voyage.

Mathematicians were already trying out much the same technique to represent figures by paths which a moving point traces on the sort of grid we now call a graph. If we make such a grid with vertical lines to show time and horizontal lines to show distance, we can easily plot Achilles' race with the tortoise. One line shows where Achilles starts and how fast he runs; another shows where the tortoise starts and how fast it runs. The point where the lines cross shows where Achilles overtakes the tortoise.

The first man to realise clearly how useful graphs can be was Rene Descartes, a great French mathematician of the seventeenth century. As a simple example of one use to which we can put them you may try solving the problem of finding x when we are told that $4x^2-4x-12=3$.

A statement of this kind tells us that one quantity equals another, so we call it an equation.

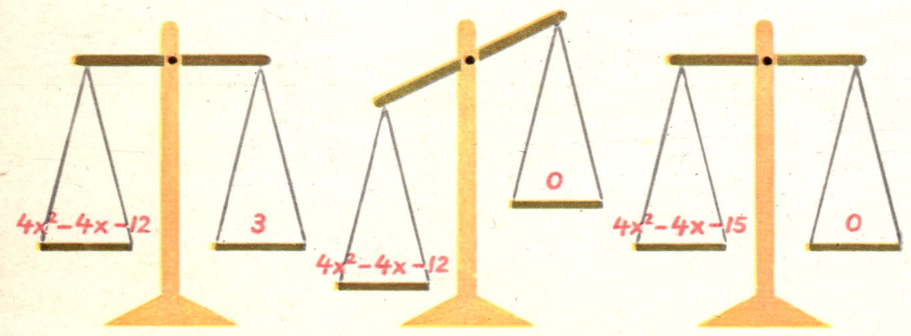

An equation keeps in balance only if we treat both sides alike.

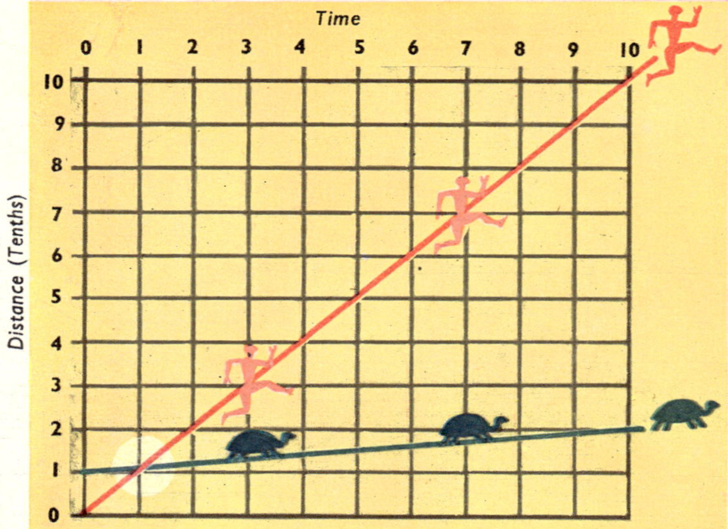

On a graph, two lines sum up Achilles' race with the tortoise.

As a first step to getting the answer, it is usual to make one side of the equation zero, but we can *keep* both sides equal only if we take the same quantity from each. We therefore take 3 from each side and re-write it as $4x^2-4x-15=0$. We now make guesses about the value of x and draw up a table to show what the right-hand side of the equation will be if each guess is correct. (In working out our table we need to remember that multiplying like signs gives a plus, multiplying unlike signs gives a minus.)

If we choose whole numbers for the values of x in our table, we find that none of them yields the right result; that is to say 0 on the right-hand side. But if we make a graph by plotting all our results as points placed vertically for successive values of x spaced equidistant horizontally, we can get a curve like a ship's course by joining each point. This curve cuts the zero line at two points. $2\frac{1}{2}$ and $-1\frac{1}{2}$. We thus see that there are two values of x which will solve our equation correctly, as is always true of this kind of equation, which we call a quadratic.

Descartes was also one of the first mathematicians to write out equations with letters and signs which we use today; but most of all, he made a closer tie between geometry and algebra than ever before. He first used algebra to state rules for drawing certain geometrical figures.

The Greeks had studied only curves one can draw with the help of compass and ruler. Descartes contended that any curve is worthy of study if we can state a rule for drawing it. We cannot draw the curve called the parabola which corresponds to the flight of the cannon-ball, if we stick to the compass and ruler recipe, but it was important for the mathematician to study such a curve in an age when the cannon could decide the fate of a nation. By the use of the graph, Descartes was able to state a rule which does enable us to draw a parabola.

The scientists of the period were becoming increasingly aware of the importance of another curve, the ellipse. With a few exceptions, such as Aristarchus and Philolaus, Greek astronomers believed that the sun moves round the earth, and until about 1540 Western Europe accepted that belief. Then Copernicus, the great Polish astronomer, revived the theory of Aristarchus, that the earth and the planets circle round the sun. During the next hundred years this theory was confirmed in broad outline by other astronomers, including Tycho Brahe, Kepler and Galileo, but Kepler discovered that the track of a planet round the sun is not exactly a circle. It is an ellipse—the figure which we now draw by moving a tightly-stretched loop of cord around two fixed pins or pegs.

In an age when accurate navigation depended more than ever on the work of the astronomer, the new geometry of Descartes made it possible to state as an algebraic formula the rule which enables us to draw an ellipse on a graph.

Value of x	*Value of $4x^2 - 4x - 15$*	*Result*
−2	16 + 8 − 15	9
−1	4 + 4 − 15	−7
0	0 − 0 − 15	−15
1	4 − 4 − 15	−15
2	16 − 8 − 15	−7
3	36 − 12 − 15	9

Points where curve cuts zero-line give correct values for x.

Loop drawn round two pegs produces an ellipse.

Uraniborg, Danish for 'Tower of Heaven', where Tycho Brahe observed heavens.

In the early air-pump, a vacuum was created by pumping water from a sealed vessel. In a vacuum, feather and stone fall at same speed.

Isaac Newton, the greatest scientist and mathematician of the Age of Discovery, gathered the threads of observation and reason, spun by so many earlier scientists, and wove them into a satisfying pattern.

From earliest times, men have studied the motions of sun, moon and stars, but Newton was the first to give a satisfactory theory of their movements. Kepler who discovered that the planets move in ellipses round the sun, could never understand why they do so. Galileo, who understood how the force of gravity explains the path of a cannon-ball, did not realise that the same force might explain the path of the planets.

Before Newton gave his explanation, an important invention had advanced knowledge beyond the level of Galileo's time. The air-pump had made it possible to experiment with falling bodies in a vacuum, and so to obtain more accurate information about gravitation. Reasoning from how we trace the flight of the cannon-ball from what we know about the behaviour of falling bodies, Descartes stated the rule that any moving body will continue to move in a straight line unless some force halts it or changes its direction.

Thus Newton's problem was not to explain why the planets keep moving. The question he tackled was why they move in a closed curve rather than in a straight line. His solution was that the force of gravity throughout the universe acts in accordance with the same laws as on our own earth. Just as the mass of the earth pulls a weight towards its central point, the mass of the sun pulls a planet towards *its* central point. In the absence of gravity, a planet, like a cannon-ball, would travel in a straight line; but the pull of the sun moves it away from that line. Newton demonstrated how the speed of the planets and the pull of the sun together keep the planets in the closed curve which they follow.

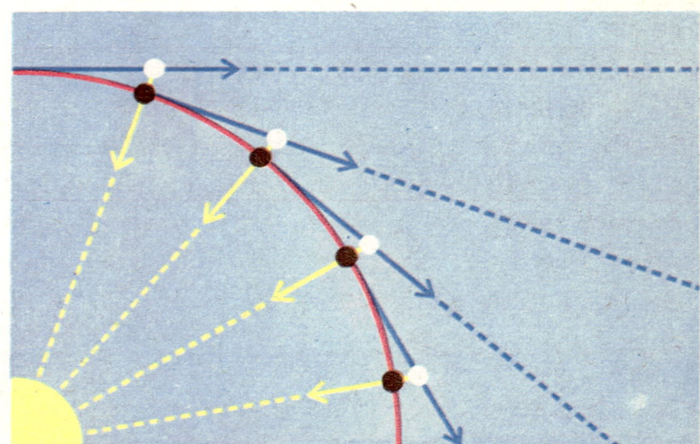

Sun's mass pulls planet steadily from straight path it would otherwise follow, so that planet travels along closed curve.

One thing which contributed to the tremendous progress in astronomy in the days of Galileo and Newton was the invention of the telescope. It seems that the first telescope was made in 1608 by a Dutch spectacle-maker named Hans Lippershey, but it was Galileo who first used a telescope

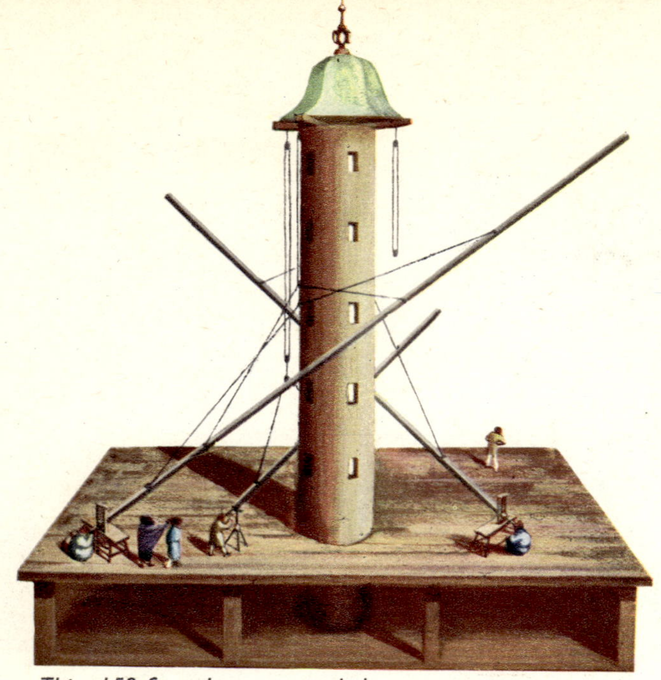

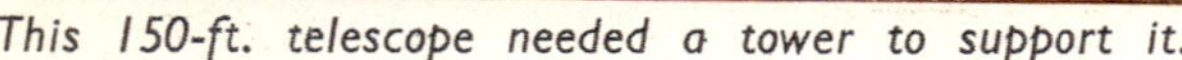

This 150-ft. telescope needed a tower to support it.

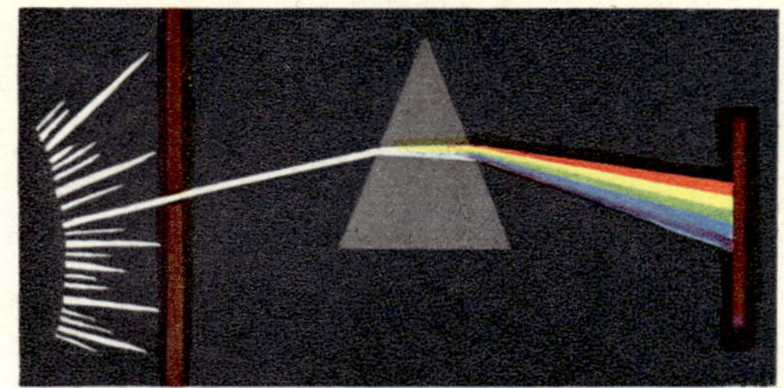

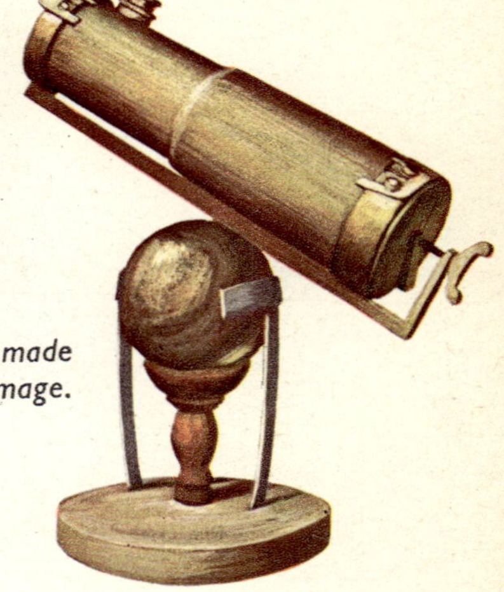

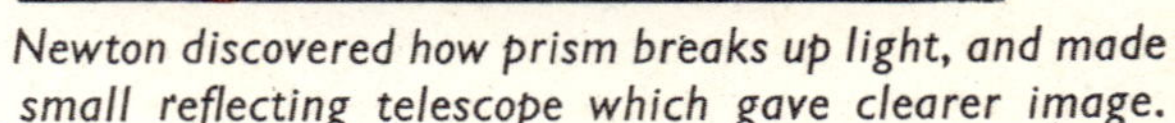

Newton discovered how prism breaks up light, and made small reflecting telescope which gave clearer image.

of his own design to study the heavens. The weakness of the early telescope was that it gave a blurred image of the object on which it was focused. Some astronomers tried to remedy this by altering the shape or position of the lenses, others by lengthening the whole instrument.

While investigating the properties of light, Newton discovered the varied coloration which results when a beam of sunlight passes through a glass prism. He realised that the light passing through the lens of Galileo's telescope behaved in the same way, thus blurring the image. He therefore designed a new telescope in which light from the object was reflected from a curved mirror on to a flat one and thence to the eye-piece, without having to pass through a lens at all.

In the days of Newton, scientific academies were being founded throughout Europe, and, more than ever before, scientists of many lands were pooling their knowledge. Thus it happened that two outstanding men, both drawing from the common pool, made the same great advance in mathematics, independently of each other and at the same time. Leibniz in Germany and Newton in England both founded a new and fruitful means of calculation called the infinitesimal calculus. It has revolutionised every branch of science which plays a part in modern industry.

Scientific academy of Newton's time

Power and Precision

For thousands of years, man has harnessed the wind to drive his sailing ships. For hundreds of years he has used the power of the wind and of fast-flowing streams to turn mill-sails and mill-wheels. Yet right up to the time of Newton and Leibniz most of the world's work – the lifting and carrying, hewing and hammering, making and mending – was still done by muscle-power. By then the need for new sources of power was becoming urgent. The miners of western Europe, and especially those of Britain, were sinking deeper shafts than ever before. Muscle-powered pumps could no longer cope with the large quantities of water which accumulated in the pits.

By the close of the seventeenth century, Denys Papin, a Frenchman, and Thomas Savery, an Englishman, had both succeeded in making crude pumps driven by steam. Within a few years Thomas Newcomen made the first steam-powered piston engine. Fifty years later James Watt fitted the steam-engine with a separate condenser, which cut down waste of heat and fuel. He also invented a means by which the steam-engine could be made to turn wheels.

During the century that followed Watt's inventions, steam-power rapidly changed the whole way of life in the western world. Industry moved away from the country cottage into the factories of huge industrial cities which sprang up near coalfields, where fuel for steam-engines was cheap and plentiful. Smoking funnels replaced white sails along the world's sea-routes. The clip-clop of the coach horse died out on the highway and made way for the rattle of steam locomotives carrying freight and passengers along the new railroads.

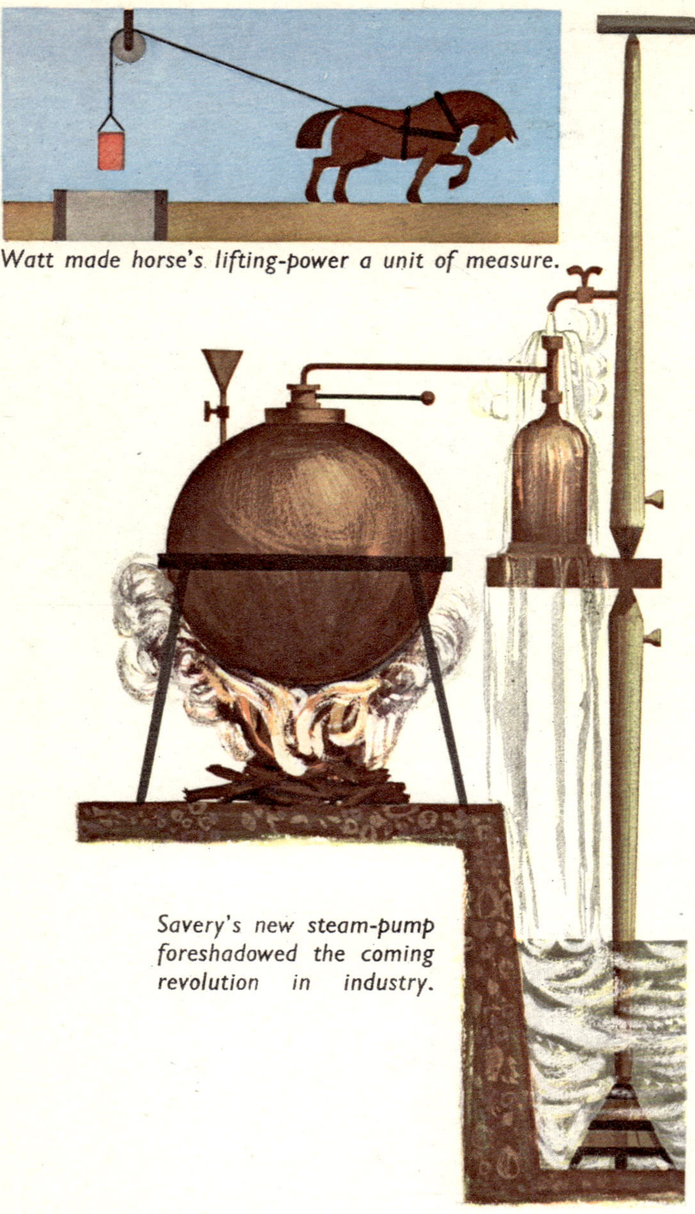

Watt made horse's lifting-power a unit of measure.

Savery's new steam-pump foreshadowed the coming revolution in industry.

Such rapid increase in the use of steam power was at first largely due to the way in which Watt and his business partner, Boulton, were able to convince customers of the usefulness and cheapness of the engines they made. They found by experiment that a strong horse can raise a 150-lb. weight, suspended over a pulley, 220 feet in one minute. If one of their engines could raise ten times that weight through the same distance in one minute, they classed it as a ten horse-power model. The customer could then compare the cost of buying fuel for such an engine with the cost of providing keep for ten horses, and usually he found that it would pay him, in the long run, to lease the engine.

It may seem strange that horse-power became a standard unit of power-measurement just at the moment when horses were losing their importance in industry, but the reason is not hard to find. New kinds of measurement are more easy to understand if based on older ones we already use. When improved oil lamps and gas lamps were taking the place of candles at the beginning of the new industrial age, the illumination they gave was at first measured in candle-power.

In the time of Watt, all steam-engines worked at much the same pressure. It was thus possible to estimate the horse-power of an engine from the size of its cylinder. As design became more varied, indicators or steam gauges came into use to measure the pressure of steam generated in the cylinder in pounds per square inch.

Many units of measurement we use today would have puzzled the engineers and scientists of Watt's time. When we speak of volts and amperes in connection with electricity, or therms and calories in connection with heat, we are using a language of precise measurement devised to meet the needs of the age of power.

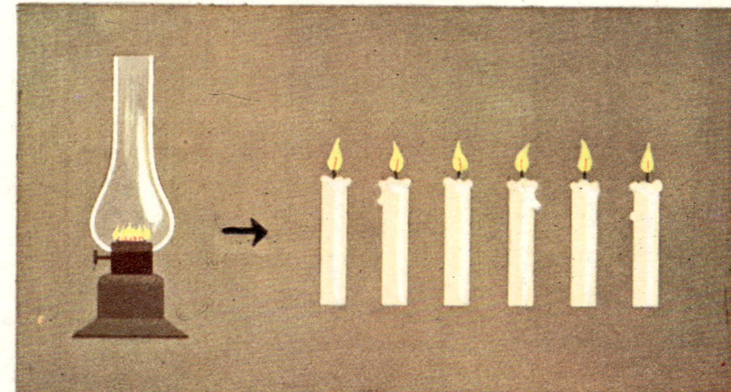

The illumination of new lamps was at first measured by the unit of illumination of the candles, which they were to replace.

Steam-gauges measured pressure in pound-per-square-inch units.

At night large towns are ablaze with light, near dawn almost in darkness. Power stations must anticipate change in power-demand.

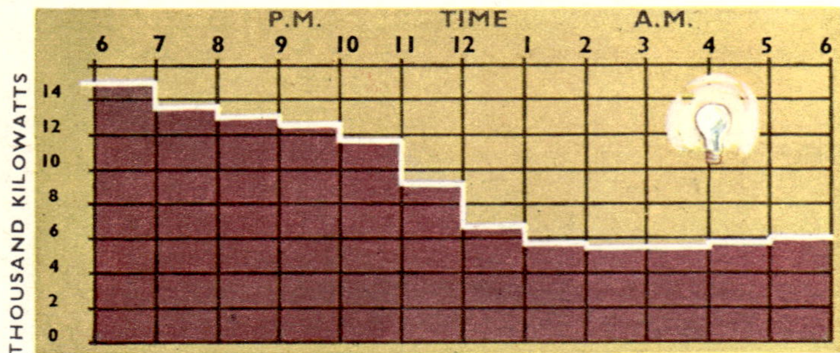

Each bar shows the power consumed in one particular hour.

In setting the world on the road to greater power, Boulton and Watt also ushered in the age of large-scale production. Boulton once wrote: It would not be worth my while to make for three counties only; but I find it well worth my while to make for all the world. The manufacturer who produces goods or services on such a scale cannot long remain content with accounts which show only his income and expenditure, profit or loss. He must plan production ahead, and to do that he needs to know the answers to a host of questions: Does the demand for his products change from season to season? Where do his goods sell best? Where and how can he improve the sales of his goods?

A record of information which may help to answer such questions is often kept in the form of simple diagrams. For example, a power station may record, by means of a bar-chart or histogram, how much electricity it supplies in a day. The height of each bar of such a chart indicates the amount of power used in one particular hour. An exporter may prepare a pie-chart, in which the

Pie-chart shows where sugar from Cuba was sold in a recent year.

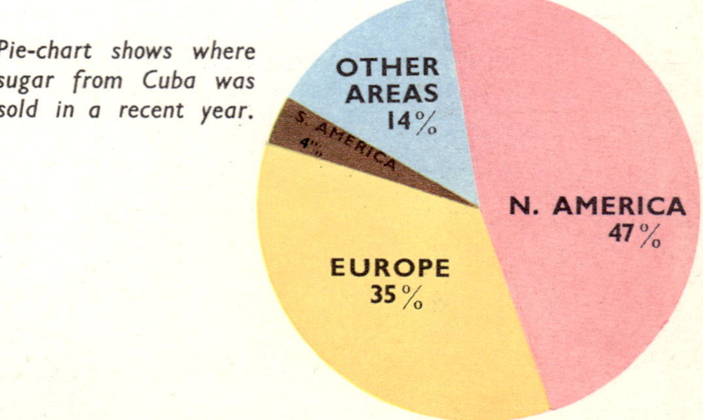

Loading sugar-cane for export.

The great change in the design of automobiles and airplanes is the result not of whim but of research and of applied mathematics.

whole area of a circle represents his total overseas sales, and the areas of various segments, or slices, represent the sales to particular regions.

Progress in accountancy is only one feature of the age of power. Perhaps a more important one is progress in design.

When we compare the shapes of automobiles or of airplanes of forty years ago with those of today we can see how great such progress has been. We may or may not prefer the new look for its own sake; but it spells greater efficiency. The streamlined design enables the modern machine to move smoothly and rapidly with a minimum expenditure of power.

Change of design has not come about by the whim of fashion. It relies on the research work of the engineer whose calculations rely on the work of the mathematician. A recent pamphlet on aerodynamics, the science which concerns itself with wind forces, wind speeds and streamlining, says: Advanced mathematical treatment, continually checked and modified by experimental research, is now an essential tool.

Thus we see that mathematics is just as closely bound up with the problems of real life today as it was when the priests of Egypt planned the great pyramids. It may need the practised eye of the aircraft-designer to detect the mathematics that lie behind the subtle curves of a modern jet-plane, but there are other modern structures which proclaim their mathematical origins as clearly as do the pyramids. When we look at the blue-print for a suspension bridge, we are clearly seeing just the kind of graph-line that Descartes might have drawn, and we recognise the finished bridge as a graph in steel.

The real-life problems of a fast-moving world are far more complex than those of ancient Egypt, when the shortest unit of time was for most purposes the hour. As the problems which crop up in the world's work have come to be more complicated, mathematics has come to be more complicated in the effort to solve them. Fortunately the mathematician of our own time has at his command aids to rapid calculation such as his predecessors never dreamed of.

The modern suspension bridge is a graph drawn in solid steel.

The mathematics of aircraft design takes airflow into account.

Modern aids enable the draughtsman of today to solve problems that would have baffled the wisest mathematicians of ancient times.

With the help of instruments which look simple, a young draughtsman or engineer's apprentice can now solve problems that would have baffled the most learned mathematicians of antiquity. With a slide-rule, much improved since Oughtred invented it in 1621, he can find the area of any circle and the square or square-root of any number with sufficient accuracy for his purpose in a few seconds. With a micrometer, he can measure the thickness of a piece of metal to within one ten-thousandth part of an inch. With a protractor he can lay out any angle with even greater accuracy than the priests of Egypt could lay out a right-angle. With the help of French curves, he can trace out graph outlines beyond the scope of the ruler-and-compass geometry of Euclid.

Small-radius compass

Steam power and electric power have freed our muscles from a great deal of hard, tiring work. New mathematical tools have also freed our minds from the drudgery of much time-consuming calculation. To re-draw a ground-plan on a scale three times larger than the original, a draughtsman of bygone times would have had to measure each line carefully and to multiply its length by three before re-drawing it. The draughtsman of today simply adjusts his proportional dividers so that the distance between one pair of points is three times as great as the distance between the other pair. When he sets one pair of points to the length of a line on his original drawing, the other pair automatically then shows what length the same line should be on the new one.

In the age of Newton, mathematicians had already equipped the astronomer and the engineer with log-tables which enabled them to turn problems of multiplication or division into the much simpler operations of addition or subtraction. In the age of power we have electronic calculators which can solve the most complicated problems of arithmetic in the twinkling of an eye.

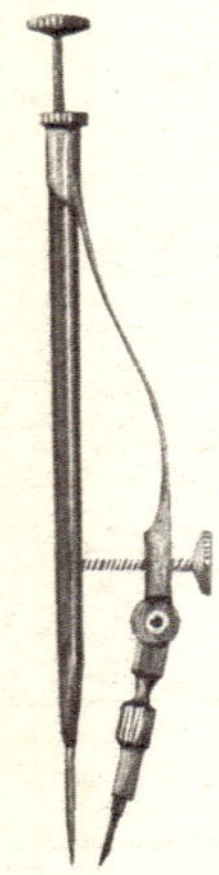

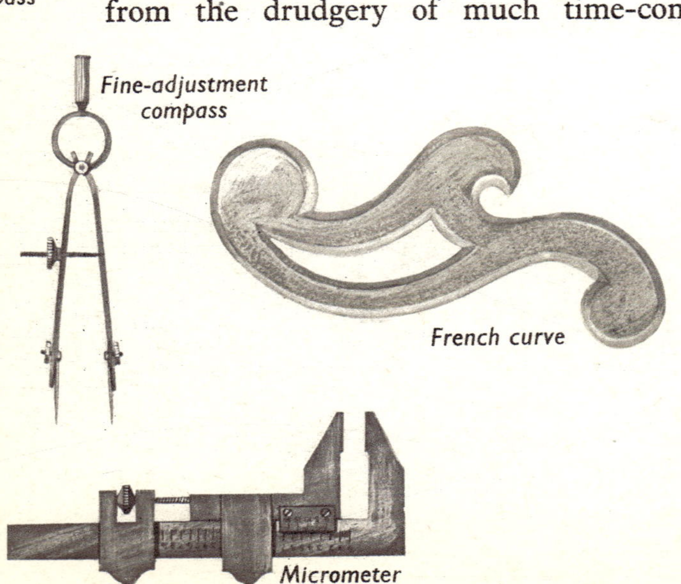
Fine-adjustment compass

French curve

Micrometer

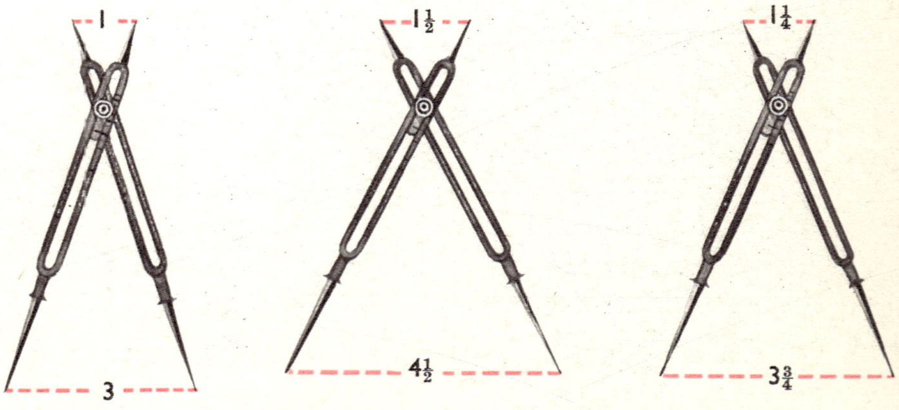

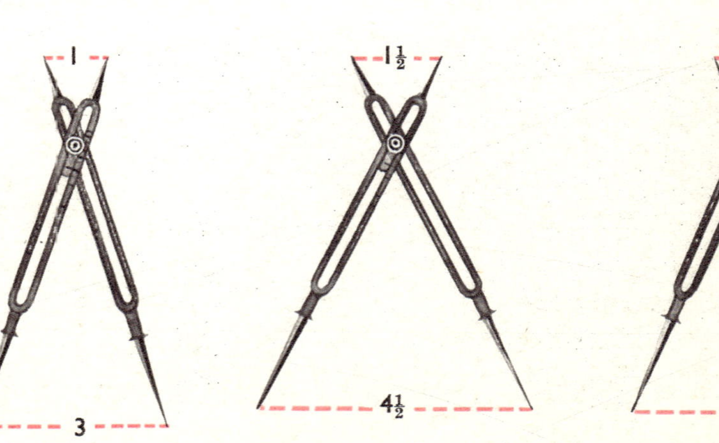

Proportional dividers embody in brass and steel the whole idea of ratio.

Of course, it would be foolish to imagine that we are wiser than our forefathers merely because we can calculate faster than they could. The very aids which enable us to do so are based on knowledge which past generations have discovered for us. If no one had ever worked out an accurate value for π, we should not now have slide-rules capable of helping us to find the area of a circle. If no one had ever learned to divide the circle into degrees, we should not now have protractors to help us to lay out angles.

Even when we use the electronic calculator we are indebted to the long-forgotten eastern merchant who first adapted number signs to the layout of the abacus. His predecessor, the temple scribe who gave to each pebble a number value ten times as great when moved one groove to the left, first gave ordinary men a clear idea of the use of a fixed base in mathematics. The electronic calculator of today still makes use of a fixed base, though it commonly employs a base of two instead of ten. With a base of ten our columns from right to left stand for ones, tens, hundreds, thousands and so on. If the base is two, they stand for ones, twos, fours, eights and so on. When we use a base of two, we can write any number with the help of only two signs, one standing for one and the other for zero. In our diagram below we use + for one and − for zero, but other signs would serve equally well.

All our modern aids to calculation are the rewards of work done in the past. But the mathematicians of the age of power are using the heritage of the past to forge new tools of scientific thought for the use of future generations.

By challenging one of the few points which Euclid took for granted, and by convincing himself that it need not be taken for granted, Karl Gauss, a great mathematician of last century, founded an entirely new system of geometry which helps the astronomer to calculate the distance of remote stars. With the help of a calculus, different from that used by Newton and Leibniz, Albert Einstein, the greatest mathematician of our own century, worked out his famous theory of relativity which helps the scientist to a better understanding of the inside of the atom and the movements of the stars. If we look at one of Einstein's equations, $M_v = \frac{M_o}{\sqrt{1-\frac{V^2}{c^2}}}$, we can see how his great work depends on the numerals and working-signs of earlier ages.

And so, step by step, progress in mathematics continues. It may well be that the future holds in store even greater discoveries than any yet made since the far-off days of the first moon-calendar.

The electronic calculator often uses the simplest base of all: 2.

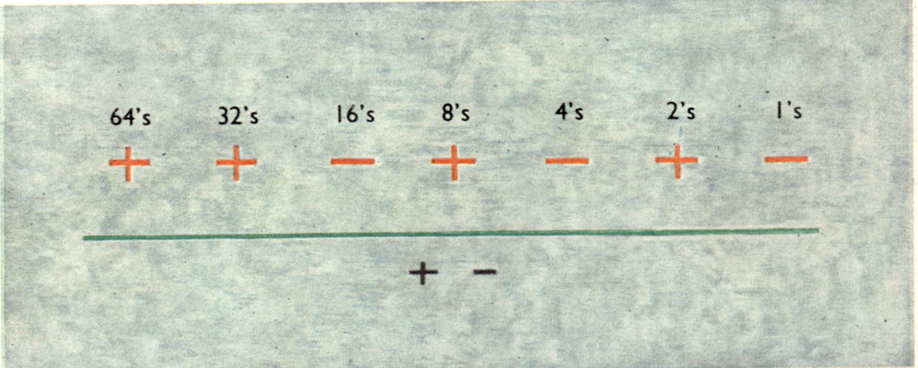

When we use a base of 2, we can write any number with two signs. In the diagram above, + stands for 1, − for 0. The number is 106.

The Beginning

25,000 B.C.
to
5000 B.C.

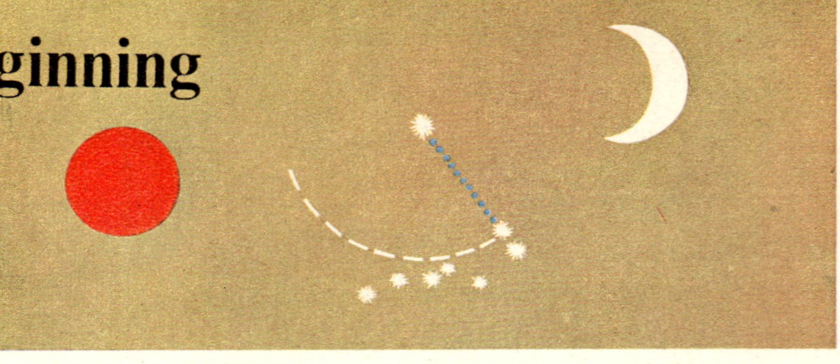

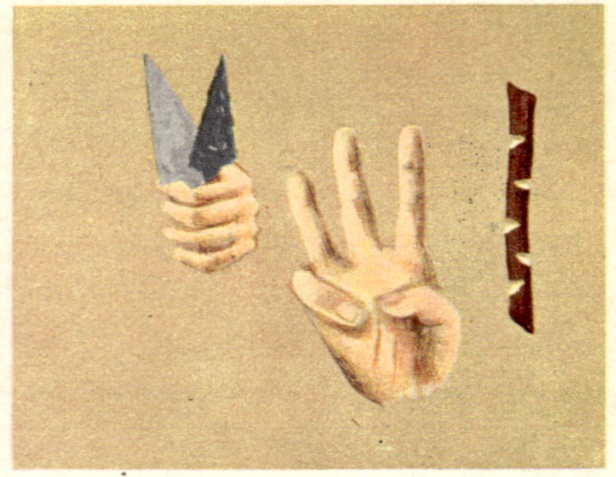

Direction-finding from stars about 23000 B.C.
Tilling the soil begins around 6000 to 5000 B.C.

Ancient Egypt

5000 B.C.
to
500 B.C.

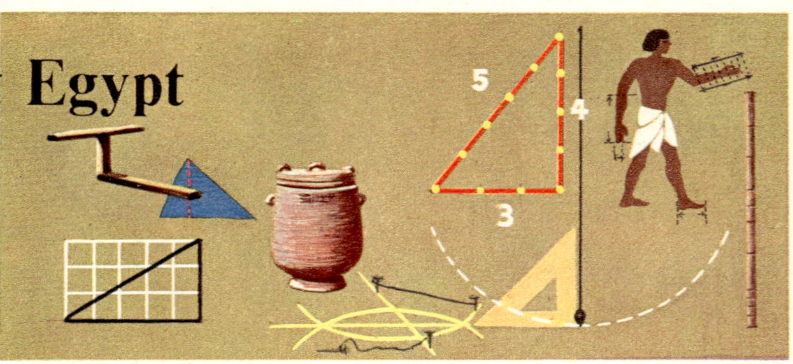

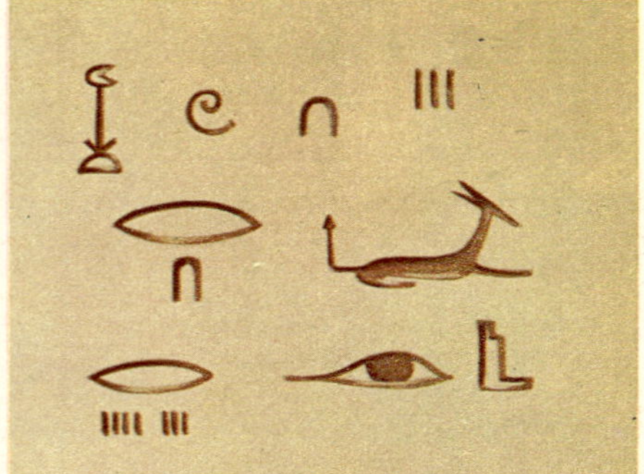

Sun-calendar possibly 4241 B.C. Great Pyramid about 2900 B.C.
Papyrus of Ahmes about 1600 B.C. First sun-dials about 1500 B.C.

Babylon and Assyria

5000 B.C.
to
500 B.C.

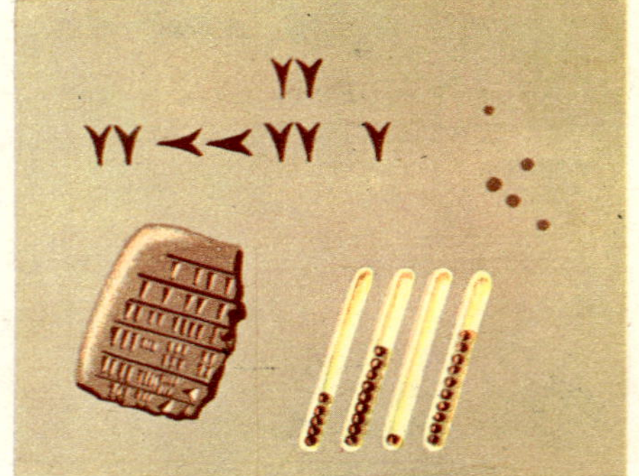

Wheels used by 5000 B.C. Tables of eclipses by 2700 B.C. Clay tablets with measures about 2400 B.C. Tables of squares about 2200 B.C. Stamped silver bars by 650 B.C.

Phoenician Voyages

1600 B.C.
to
500 B.C.

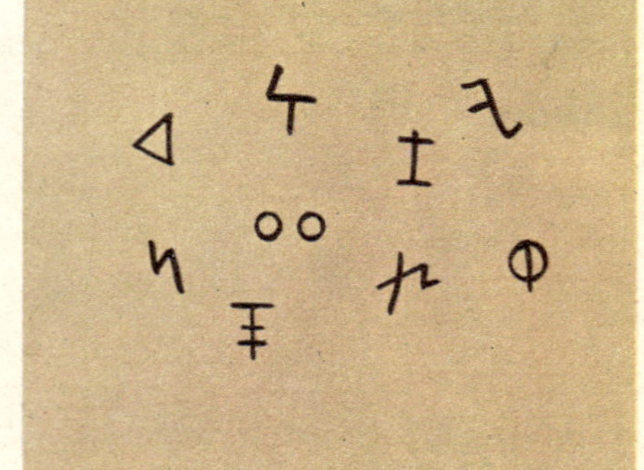

Carthage founded 813 B.C. Voyage around African coast 700 B.C. Alphabetic inscriptions by 600 B.C.

Greece and Rome

800 B.C.
to
450 A.D.

Thales in Egypt by 600 B.C. Pythagoras's Brotherhood 530 B.C. Alexandria founded 332 B.C. Euclid's Elements 300 B.C. Archimedes 287–212 B.C. Roman Empire in its prime by 50 B.C.

Moslem Empire

640 A.D.
to
1250 A.D.

Moslems conquer Persia and Egypt by 640 A.D., Spain about 720. Baghdad founded about 760. Hindu numerals in use by 766. Universities in Spain by 800. Adelard's translations 1120.

Western Europe

1250 A.D.
to
1775 A.D.

New numerals widely used by 1400. First printed arithmetics by 1480. Columbus in New World 1492. Galileo 1564–1642. Descartes 1596–1650. Newton 1642–1727. Leibniz 1646–1716.

The Industrial World

1775 A.D
to
Today

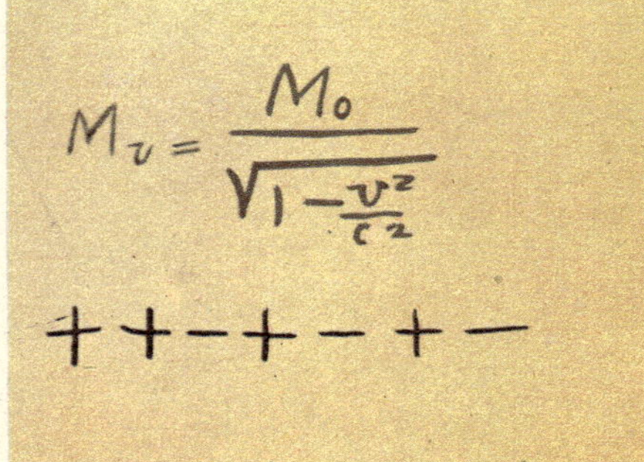

Watt's engine in use by 1780. Gauss 1777–1855. Gas street lights 1805. Steam trains 1825. Electric lights 1876. Automobiles 1885. Wright brothers' flight 1903. Einstein 1879–1955.